THE WINTER OF THE WOLF
OF THE WOLF
GROWING UP UNDER STALIN AND HITLER

BY WOLODYMYR PAPUCA

Published by Book of My Life Ltd
20–22 Wenlock Road
London
N1 7GU
0845 643 9423
bookofmylife.co.uk

Book OF MY Life

CONTENTS

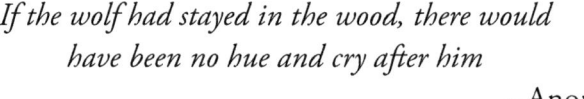

If the wolf had stayed in the wood, there would have been no hue and cry after him

– Anon

AUTHOR'S FOREWORD

I intend this memoir for my son Nick and my six grandchildren, Alex, Ben, Charlotte, Josephine, Max and Fay. It has taken me many years to reveal these incidents from my early life because I was brought up in a culture in which people could, and often did, disappear as a consequence of a political indiscretion, even if very minor. As you read my tale you will see that I had to adapt again and again in order to survive. My motivation to continue was overwhelming. Even so, I was lucky to be preserved when so many died, some of them relatives and close friends. I never gave up. Whatever your ambitions in life, draw strength from your family history.

Wolodymyr Papuca, 2016

EDITORIAL INTRODUCTION

This true story tells of Wolodymyr Papuca, whose Ukrainian childhood and early adulthood were entangled in the rival ideologies of communism and Nazism. Inimical to both, he was engulfed by the war between them yet survived, eventually to reach England and to become a British citizen.

The events described in the account which follows require to be seen in the context of Ukrainian history and of the political turbulence of their time. That history and those politics are inordinately complex; they are here, necessarily, greatly simplified.

Ukraine is, in area, the largest wholly European country, albeit its boundaries have been, and continue to be, repeatedly altered (Map 1). At the outbreak of the First World War in 1914, Ukraine did not exist as a nation. Most of the territory constituting modern Ukraine was then part of the Tsarist Russian Empire.

However, to the west lay a region (broadly Galicia, with Lvov near its middle), administered by the Austro-Hungarian (Habsburg) Empire. Ukrainians were thus divided between two great opposing powers. In the First World War, as many as 3.5 million Ukrainians are said to have served with the Imperial Russian Army against some 250,000 with the Austro-Hungarian Army.

The Tsarist Empire collapsed with the Russian revolutions of 1917. In March 1918, the Treaty of Brest-Litovsk led to the cessation of hostilities between what had become Bolshevik Russia and the Central Powers (predominantly Germany and Austria-Hungary). According to that treaty, Ukraine was to become an independent state under the protection of Germany. However, the defeat of the Central Powers in November 1918 led to abrogation of the Treaty of Brest-Litovsk.

By then the Russian Civil War was raging. In that war, the principal combatant groups were the Red Army, fighting for the Bolshevik form of socialism (communism), set against the White Army, which comprised diverse interests, variously favouring monarchism, capitalism and alternative forms of socialism.

The Red Army effectively defeated the White armed forces of South Russia in Ukraine in 1919. Some surviving remnants of the White Army were subsequently beaten in Crimea and were evacuated in 1920.

The Russian Civil War devastated Ukraine. Notions of national independence for Ukraine faded, and it became a founding constituent state of Soviet Russia (USSR) in 1922. Soviet leadership initially encouraged a national renaissance in Ukrainian culture and language, but those policies were sharply reversed when Stalin took control of the Communist Party in 1924. From the late 1920s, Ukraine was involved in Soviet industrialisation. Concurrently, agricultural collectivisation was implemented and enforced by both regular troops and secret police (Cheka). Agricultural productivity decreased markedly, and millions starved to death in the great famine (Holodomor). That famine was well under way in the 1920s and reached a peak in 1932 and 1933.

These were the circumstances leading up to, and accompanying, the present personal story, which opens in March 1929.

I have so far as possible kept my editorial interventions and observations to the minimum. The wording of the following text is essentially as told by the author.

Professor J Ian S Robertson

Wrapped up in furs, I held tightly to my mother. She cradled my baby sister Anna, born just two months earlier, keeping her close while my father drove the two horses on through the snowy night, pushing the animals to their limit, faster and faster. I closed my eyes and listened to the crack of the whip, the rhythm of the horses' hooves and the swish of the sledge. From far away, I heard the eerie howl of hungry wolves. I prayed that they would not attack the horses as they had often done in the past. I was four years old. This was the first time that I was forced to flee for my life.

1
INTO THE SNOW

My earliest memory is of snow, soft pure white snow falling so thickly and so fast that it buried our wooden one-storey home and my father had to dig a trench so that we could get out. Snow was not unusual in the village where I was born—Falenko, about 100 kilometres to the west of Merefa and Kharkov in eastern Ukraine (Map 2). Poltava was the nearest sizeable town, about 30 kilometres away to the south-west.

The Papuca family had a history going back to the 1700s in the Falenko area. In earlier generations, they contributed a considerable sum of money to build a church to serve 300 people. Our surname then was spelt Papucia. It would be changed after the Second World War to Papuca, which is like the Polish word for parrot.

My father Petro was the youngest of three brothers, and he also had a sister called Domka. The brothers lived in a cluster of houses on the eastern side of the village. The eldest, Pavlo, was a priest and had a big stone house. The middle brother, Konstantin, owned a brickworks and a sugar beet farm. His was a large brick single story house. We didn't have any other neighbours. Our road led to the centre of Falenko, where there were shops either side of the street and a village council building.

My mother, Maria, was extremely pretty, very soft, a little plump and usually wore her hair tied up in a bun. As she had been brought up on a farm, she was an expert in raising and managing animals. Once, I tried to ride a horse. I slid down the animal's neck and never tried again. But Mother was excellent at both riding and driving horses.

My parents had an arranged marriage, which was the custom at that time in Ukraine. My mother was just 15 when she married my father, who was 12 years her senior, and 20 when I was born in March 1925. Anna Petrona, my sister, was born four years later.

A rich farmer, my father had over 200 hectares of agricultural land for growing corn and a windmill for threshing, preparing and grinding the grain. He was also involved in roasting sunflower seeds and squeezing them to extract the oil. He employed seven people. As a sideline, my father ran a shop in the village, which sold clothes. Whenever he needed new stock, he would journey to Merefa, near Kharkov, taking two horses and the sledge. When he came back late in the evening, wolves would often try to attack the horses. His whip was always at the ready to drive them away.

Father was a strong man physically. Always clean-shaven, he wore his brown hair brushed forwards, although he started to lose some of it as he aged. In winter, he would wear a thick cap with ear flaps to keep out the cold. He was strict with me and a bit like me in character because there were two sides to him: one was kind and loving, the other was more temperamental.

Our house was similar to a Scandinavian ski lodge. Its walls were constructed from large wooden logs infilled with clay, and the roof was thatched with straw. Although all the rooms were on one level, the house had a large floor area. There were four bedrooms. Outside was a big pond full of carp; a well; an orchard with apples, pears, plums and cherries; and fields with horses and cattle.

In the yard was a huge dog which was kept on a chain about 25 metres from the house to guard the property and the barns. He was really friendly to me, and I loved to play with him and ride him like a pony. One day, I ran outside to play with the dog but found him lying on the ground, cold and stiff. Some thieves had come to steal from our outbuildings in the night and had given him poisoned meat to silence him. I cried for a long time.

Mostly I had a happy time. There was a problem though. At that time Ukraine was part of the new Soviet Union (USSR). During the civil war that followed the Russian revolutions of 1917, my family had been on the side of the White Army. The Bolsheviks (later called communists), led by Lenin, were known as the Red Army. The Bolsheviks were victorious and then persecuted those who had sympathised with the White Army. Many had their houses confiscated and ownership transferred to the workers (the proletariat).

When Stalin took over after Lenin died in 1924, things got worse, much worse. My father and his brothers were kulaks (landowners), and Stalin wanted to eradicate this class from Ukraine. The Cheka was Stalin's secret police force, forerunner of the KGB, although its so-called secrecy was limited: The operatives, the Chekists, were seen everywhere in their distinctive long black leather coats. Each also wore a black felt hat with ear flaps and a prominent red star. Their visibility was deliberate: it was Stalin's show of strength.

The Soviet Union was at that time a land of whispers and distrust. Everyone knew there were informers listening in on conversations which could then be reported to the Chekists. The Chekists' word was law. If an informer reported you to the Cheka, there was no judge and no trial. You were sent promptly to a Gulag forced-labour prison camp. Most of these were in remote, sparsely populated areas of north-eastern Siberia, which is where the expression 'sent to Siberia' comes from. Once there, you were kept behind barbed wire, guarded by dogs and police, and forced to work for nothing. Most victims were never seen again. Those sent to the camps were often clever people, intellectuals who could make trouble for the communists. A person could be arrested for making an innocent comment that was thought to be contrary to the communist spirit; that's all it took.

This is why my parents never told me who my relatives were when I was growing up. It might sound strange but they thought it best I did not know so that I could never accidentally say something that could be used against my relations. "Keep your mouth shut," my father would order.

People I didn't know sometimes spent the night at our house.

"Who are these people?" I asked my mother.

"Oh, just friends of your father," she would say, or, "Oh, only people who work with your father." Later, during the German occupation, she told me that they were really our relatives. There were in the family teachers, an artist and a writer, but I never met them. Some of my relatives were killed by the Cheka. I don't know who or how many.

I knew comparatively little about my grandparents. My father's father had owned a large sugar plantation outside Chutove, on the road between Poltava and Kharkov. He was a strong man who was said when young to have wrestled with bulls. One day he had a row with someone, and when he arrived home he had a heart attack and died.

My mother's parents had a German name, Kramer, and lived just 20 kilometres away. Sadly, we never had the opportunity to visit them. My maternal grandfather, Theodor, worked for the council. He had two daughters, including my mother, and a son.

My father's life and property, and that of his brothers, were thus already in jeopardy. Stalin then instigated a much greater horror. Ukraine was long known as the Bread Basket of Europe because of its fertile agricultural lands, which Stalin was determined to exploit. He moved many thousands of Ukrainians to Siberia and brought Russians in to take their place. Then the land was taken over and collective farms created. The remaining Ukrainians were forced to work on these farms without pay. Most of the produce was taken by the state and household food was often confiscated. Population movement was restricted. These policies led to mass starvation known as the Holodomor. This was well advanced by the late 1920s and reached a peak in 1932 and 1933. Between 5 and 7 million people, most of whom were ethnic Ukrainians, are estimated to have died in this man-made famine.

At first, my family was not directly affected because we were still living at our farm. However, there were dwindling amounts of food in the shops. People sold their jewellery, wedding rings, clothes and anything they had to get money in order to buy something—anything—to eat.

"Stay where I can see you, Wolodymyr, or you'll be taken away and put in the pot," my mother reminded me every time I ventured outside. This wasn't a fairy tale invented to scare little children; it was a real danger. The famine was so severe that people had resorted to unthinkable measures: some children and young people really were kidnapped and killed for their flesh, which was sold on the open market. My mother was terrified that my baby sister Anna or I would be taken. The fear was drummed into us, and I was only ever allowed to play right outside the house while we lived in Falenko. Because of this I had a shortage of childhood friends.

In 1927 my Uncle Konstantin, whose sugar beet land had already been confiscated by Stalin's men, suddenly disappeared. The Chekists simply took him in the night. A year later, my Uncle Pavlo was also sent to Siberia and his house was seized.

My father knew it was only a matter of time before he too was taken. Then, in March 1929, with the winter snow still thick on the ground, he had a tip-off from someone on the village council that the Chekists were coming that night to take our property and arrest him. Straightaway, my father prepared two horses. Then he bundled my mother, my baby sister and me into the sledge. There was no time to pack, not even my favourite toy, before we set off into the darkness.

2

THE COMMUNIST IDEAL

I remember little about the long journey, except the fear that the Chekists, in their long black coats, would catch us and do horrible things to my father. I do know that Father was determined to escape, and he had a plan.

We headed for the town of Horlivka, about 300 kilometres away towards the city of Donetsk, where a relative named Shevchenko lived (Map 3). He was the chief engineer for the city's transmitter, and he gave us shelter in his home. Shevchenko then found a job for my father at the coal-fired power station in nearby Kadiyevka.

It was all so different in Kadiyevka. We'd been living on a peaceful farm. Now we were living in the noisy, smelly industrial Donets Basin (Donbas) region. There were coal mines and metalwork factories everywhere, and the racket continued all night. The sky looked like it was on fire, burning with bright white flames when the steel was produced. Near the steel plant, the water was so hot that people did their washing in it; it was far too hot for little boys to swim in though.

The city was divided up into sections: coal miners lived in one area, the water filtration people in another, and so on. In the east, there were chemical factories, and no grass would grow because of pollution. Of all the districts, that of the coal miners was the worst. Life expectancy there was short.

The first place we lived in was a two-storey block of flats provided for the power-station workers. It was in the western part of the city, where the air was relatively clean.

There were several such blocks approximately 300 metres apart; altogether about 50 families lived in our area. We had a lower-floor flat with two bedrooms, a dining room, a kitchen and a storage area. My sister slept in Mother's room and I was in Father's. Every family also had a small chalet. In ours we had another kitchen. There was also a communal kitchen used mainly for bread making. There was no lavatory inside. Instead, there were communal toilets in a long shed. It took me a while to get used to the horrible smell of human waste and carbolic acid.

In the middle of the blocks were big cellars, each shared between six families. Vegetables such as potatoes and gherkins from the collective farms were stored there. There was another large building for coal and wood. Other communal sheds housed various domestic animals. We only had to buy milk and sugar.

There were no refrigerators, although we did have electricity. Entertainment at home was provided by the state in the form of music, which was transmitted via loudspeakers in our flat—just one way the state controlled the population. There were coal fires, a stove and a system of pipes which provided underfloor heating. In another wooden communal building, there were metal tubs with washboards where Mother did the laundry.

We didn't have a bathroom. In the winter we boiled water for the bath—a metal container in which we'd sit and wash once a week. It was easier in the summer because we could wash outside in the communal showers with water heated by the sun. The men could use the showers from two to three in the afternoon; from five until six it was the women's turn. Often, I would look through the holes in the wood to spy on the girls.

My mother kept about 20 chickens and a pig. We had two pigs a year, but we were required to give the skin and a quarter of the meat to the state. When the pig was fattened up, someone would come to kill it, then Mother cut it all up and placed it in a big barrel with salt. On top of the salt she put a layer of lard to protect the meat. She made salami using the pig's intestines for the skins. Nothing was wasted.

Our neighbour kept a turkey. I often played with it and teased it by attaching a corn-on-the-cob to a string and then pulling it when the turkey had it in its beak. Then it would run after me and try to peck me. I liked animals. Sadly, I had little time to help Mother with the pig though because if I wasn't doing well in school, I would be in trouble with Father.

At harvest time, there was much for my mother to do, and she was resourceful. She put sauerkraut, gherkins and salted apples into barrels to preserve them over the winter. There was an abundance of fruit, including apples, cherries, pears, raspberries and plums. Mother would lay out the fruit on top of a tarpaulin on the ground and let the sun dry it. It would then be cut up into slices, strung on to a cord and hung up to dry. Boiled up with water and sugar, this dried fruit could make a tasty compote dessert.

The lovely aroma of food being cooked wafted through the flat. My mother baked our bread— huge round white loaves that would each last for several days. When it was my sister's or my birthday, Mother would bake a special pastry.

Soon a replacement was provided for the toys I'd left in Falenko in the form of a big wooden horse on wheels that I could sit on. I also had a small metal train which I could pull along with a string. One birthday, I fell over and cut myself while playing with the train. I still have the scar on my leg.

Most of the adults drank kvass, which is similar to beer and made of dry bread or rye mixed and fermented with water. We children drank water from a communal tap outside the flats. In winter, if the water was frozen, we'd have to put a bucket of snow on the stove to melt. Eating ice caused me lots of trouble with my teeth aching.

The winters in Ukraine could be harsh and lasted from November to March. If it was minus 20°C, we were not supposed to go to school because a child could easily freeze to death walking there and back. When it was as cold as that, people would smear goose fat on their faces if they needed to leave their homes. Rarely, temperatures fell as low as minus 40°C.

When I had to leave the flat in the freezing weather, my mother wrapped me up in long johns, thick jumpers and padded trousers. I had valenki—special boots made of felt that were two or more centimetres thick and were worn with rubber galoshes on top. I'd also wear a thick fur coat that came down to my feet.

Winter had usually ended by April, and people started hoeing and planting seeds in May. They used horse manure to fertilise the soil. There was plenty of that about because in town the vehicles were mostly horse-drawn. There were some tractors and one car, although only the communist official was permitted to drive that. In the warmer months, the smell from horse manure hung in the air.

Although the winters were cold, summers were hot. In summer, I wore shorts and little else. Often I would go barefoot. At that time of year, it was often too hot to use the flat. We'd stay in the chalet instead. There was a cooker in one room; the other big room was for sitting and dining in. August was when the temperatures were at their highest—up to 45°C; before the harvest, if you put an egg on the metal part of a tractor, you could fry it. It was so hot that people stopped work at about one o'clock. They started again at five or six and worked until ten o'clock or midnight.

In the countryside, people continued to suffer from hunger. In Kadiyevka, there were special shops where you could exchange jewellery for money to buy food with. Everyone sold their valuables there. Later on, my mother would have to sell everything, even her engagement ring, just to survive.

Even though we had moved to the city, she still worried that my sister or I would be snatched and killed and our flesh sold for meat. I never saw it happen, although I was sure it did.

"Don't go, Wolodymyr," my mother would plead when I wanted to go out to play. Happily, it was more difficult for children to be stolen in the town because there were many people about. There was a certain safety in numbers. Lots of children played outside in the streets. In the field nearby, my friends and I used to try to catch a type of animal called a suslik, a ground squirrel that looks a bit like a rat. We would throw a bucket of water down the burrow, block all the holes except one forcing the animals out, and then we caught them. We would sell them for their skins.

All religion was officially banned under communism. You could never admit you were religious or you would not get a job. It's probably why my uncle, a priest, was sent to Siberia. Instead of Christmas, we celebrated New Year. Everyone had a ten-day holiday and there was lots of music, singing and dancing; skating on an ice rink; and throwing coins at the doors. The communists also celebrated International Workers' Day on 1 May, when everyone would get drunk on vodka.

Every Sunday at eight in the morning, a brass band would start to play in the street. This was on the back of a lorry full of tools, spades and brushes and was a reminder to everyone aged about 16 or over—men and women—that they were required to spend about five hours working for the community every week. No one was paid for this work. Everyone did it anyway. If you refused, you would be in trouble. My parents had to do this community work while I stayed at home with my little sister. The brass band played while they worked, and the people constructed roads, public gardens, entertainment venues and sports grounds.

Our communist rulers were strict in insisting that no one left the country. At the border between Ukraine and Poland, for example, were 20 kilometres of no-man's-land, ploughed every day and raked. Each morning, this zone was checked to see if there were any footprints left by people trying to escape.

My father was authoritarian, and I learned to accept the good and bad things in life. He never hit my sister. I was more mischievous. If I accidentally broke wind, he would beat me and put me in a corner on my knees for two hours as a punishment. Two painful hours facing the wall just for that. My mother often tried to protect me from my father, and she was beaten a little too.

When we first moved to the city, Father attended night school for five years to study accountancy. This education was free, courtesy of the Communist Party. Having been a prosperous farmer, Father was determined to take any opportunities offered and make the communist system work for us in order to survive. "As long as we keep quiet, we will be safe," he told me. By then I was accustomed to keeping quiet.

The Chekists never did catch up with us; presumably, they were content with taking over all of Father's property. The Russians knew there were lots of former kulaks in the city, but they needed them to run the country because they were educated and skilled.

Although my family did not believe in communism, we had no choice but to go along with it. If we kept our mouths shut and knuckled down, there was a chance that we would be all right.

3
A YOUNG COMMUNIST

"Wolodymyr, you must work hard and get top marks in all your subjects," said my father regularly. He was keen for me to do well in everything at school because he knew that whoever scored the highest marks had the best opportunities in life. If I was a bit below the required standard, I would get a smack and he would pay for a teacher to give me extra tuition. Happily, this didn't happen often, although I struggled with languages more than other subjects.

At home, we had books like Jules Verne's *Around the World in 80 Days* and Dumas's *The Three Musketeers*. Sadly, I never really had much time to read because I had so much homework. We had to write out the alphabet over and over just to practise our handwriting. There would be a big A and a small A, then B and so on, pages and pages of them.

Although my sister attended a kindergarten before starting school proper, I don't remember doing the same. Between the ages of eight and 15, education was paid for by the state. In 1933, aged eight, I started at a Ukrainian school. I had to walk about a kilometre to get there because it was in the west of the city, next to the area where the water filtration people lived. I had to pass through the outskirts of the coal mining district on the way.

About a year after I started school, Father qualified as a chief accountant and was given a promotion at the power station. With a higher position, he was entitled to a better house, and we were transferred to a bungalow with a big garden in a quieter area. The bungalow was made of stone with two steps outside the front door. We had an outside tap and running water inside too. It was semi-detached, and we shared the cellar with our neighbours, who were teachers. I was excited to have a bedroom to myself, and my sister did too.

Following his promotion, Father applied to join the Communist Party to make life easier for us. After passing a test, he was accepted. From then on, he had good connections with some of the Party officials. My father and his new friends played bridge or another card game called preferans. They came to our house on Saturdays, about once a month, and brought luxury foods with them such as French and

Swiss cheeses, salami, brandy and caviar. Ordinary people couldn't get this kind of food; it came from a special shop which only communist officials could use. If there was any food left over, Anna and I were allowed to eat it.

"Now you must become a Young Communist," said my father shortly after he joined the Party. I was eight years old. I was given a pass and badge and a red neckerchief to wear as the Young Communists were similar to the Scouts. It wasn't that I wanted to join, but if I hadn't it would have looked suspicious and people would have asked questions. All my friends signed up as well. We didn't necessarily believe in what they were saying; we joined to make life easier.

If I was awarded a good mark during the year, my father would reward me with a month, sometimes two, at the summer youth camp in what was known as the Black Forest (Map 3). I started going from about the age of eight. The camp wasn't far from Donetsk and the River Donets. There were no more than about 40 or 50 children altogether. Only people who had responsible jobs and were well paid could afford to send their children there.

Donetsk is warm in the summer, and I used to love the Black Forest camp because of the fresh air and natural surroundings. It reminded me of the countryside around the farm where I was born. My mother was sent to do the cooking for the summer camps. We stayed in a chalet there, and my sister Anna went too. There were lots of animals in the woods and along the river, including small brown bears and wild boar, although they never came into the camp. In the forest, there were pigeons and sparrows, as well as woodpeckers and cuckoos, which made lots of noise.

The camp had a teacher for everything—sports, music, dancing and swimming. At seven in the morning, somebody would raise the flag and we had to exercise—running for half an hour. Then we had to wash. At nine in the evening, the national anthem was played on the accordion and the flag was lowered.

In the Black Forest, the teachers taught us all about the natural world, including the names of various wild flowers, and we would collect berries.

I joined the fishing club, and we tried to catch catfish in the lake. These fish had whiskers and could be up to two metres long. Some of the boys would take out a rowing boat. They'd catch a catfish with a rod and then hold on to it while the great fish pulled the boat along until it became too tired to swim any more.

Each morning from 11 o'clock, everyone had to swim for an hour. There were four instructors who put flags in the Donets River, and told us not to swim beyond them because there the water could take us away. We had special cotton swimming trunks. We never had proper lessons. They just threw us into the water and we had to learn to survive. That's the way they trained us—sink or swim. I also swam in the evenings there. I preferred to lie on my back because I didn't have much strength.

I had a problem with my lungs and was often unwell. The communist health system was free and there was a big clinic with lots of doctors. I could have gone to the hospital. Instead, my father decided to pay for me to see a professor whom he knew through the card games played in our home.

Father suffered with stomach problems. To improve his health, he would sometimes travel to the Caucasus for several weeks, paid for by the Party. It was a holiday for him, but we weren't allowed to accompany him.

There were many ethnic groups in Ukraine and some 17 different languages, the only common one being Russian. Everyone had to speak Russian, whether you were Russian, Ukrainian, Greek or Polish.

In 1937, at the age of 12, I was sent to the big Russian school, which was really modern. There were 700 pupils—boys and girls—and lots of well-qualified teachers. The school offered a good education. I travelled there by tram as it was about two kilometres from my home.

We started at eight and finished at one, and we were always sent home with a lot of homework. I was good at science. It was only languages I had difficulty with, although I could already speak Russian and Ukrainian. We learned German in school because all the factories and machinery had been built by Germans, making it an important skill. I also learned a little English and Latin. Girls seemed to be cleverer than boys at languages.

We had music lessons at school and we were taught to play the violin. Do-Re-Mi-Fa-Sol-La-Ti were the notes. I couldn't work out the difference so I copied from the boy in front of me. Unfortunately, he was wrong and so was I, and the teacher spotted me playing the wrong notes. We both failed. I also did a bit of Turkish Cossack dancing at school wearing silk boots. I wasn't very good because I never had time to practise.

Chess was another subject that we were taught in school. When I was about 14 or 15, I won a prize for chess. I came first, and the reward was a trip to the youth camp. In all subjects, the girls and boys were mixed up. There was no difference between men and women in the Soviet Union. Women could be soldiers, they drove tanks and even flew planes.

Once, in a German lesson, I made a paper aeroplane. My classmates and I giggled as it flew around the room. Then I watched in horror as my little plane bounced off the ceiling and hit the teacher on the head. I was suspended from school for three days. For that, my father hit me with a belt for two hours. He could be cruel, and I used to get lots of bruises.

That wasn't the worst thing I ever did. When I was about 14, everyone was in a gang. There were about 20 lads in each gang, and at weekends we often fought the coal miners with catapults and cast-iron ball bearings. The police had to separate us.

On one of the local sports pitches, there was a kiosk selling soft drinks. "Let's steal some drinks," said one of my gang one day. "Wolodymyr, you can be lookout." The kiosk was on stilts, and some boys in my gang hid underneath until it was closed. Then one of the gang unlocked it to steal the drinks. Although I was about 100 metres away, I was the only one to be grabbed by the police. The rest ran away.

At the police station, they took off my belt and I was put in a cell for three days. I felt miserable, frightened and humiliated; I had to hold up my trousers when I walked around; and the story made it into the newspaper. It was even worse when I was released. My father gave me a real belting. I was black and blue all over. I had only joined in with this gang for a bit of fun. After I was arrested, I decided not to get involved any more.

In Kadiyevka, there was a huge park for the community with a football field, volleyball and netball courts, and a skittle alley. At weekends, they played brass band music in the bandstand. In one area of the park, there were lots of trees. Young people and courting couples would sneak in there to make love. My friends and I were naturally curious about these things. One day, we were there taking a quick peek when a man spotted us and chased us away. We had to run for our lives.

Other state-run entertainments included a big cinema, enough for several hundred people, where they sometimes showed American films. Once, I saw a Charlie Chaplin picture there. Films were on at weekends mostly all year round, although I never had much time to see them because my father expected me to study hard. Another part of the building contained the library, which was free. It had a good range of books, including a children's section. I saw my cousin Alexander there once looking at the sex books. He was five or six years older than me.

Back then, carbide was used in lights. If you put carbide in water, a gas is produced which can create an explosion. At the age of 12 or 13, my friends and I used to play with these carbide lamps in a field, making mini blasts for fun. In the summer, we would make our way to a nearby lake to swim and fish. When it snowed in the winter, we loved ice skating, cross-country skiing and tobogganing. The skis and sticks were all home-made from local wood without any kind of bindings.

At 14, I had dreams of being a captain in the merchant navy at Odessa, 500 kilometres away. I hardly knew the wider countryside because I'd never travelled and I wanted to get away. From the age of 16, to travel from one place to another, you needed a permit. Without one, you could be arrested.

"No," said my father when I told him my plans. "Odessa is too far. There is a medical school in Donetz and a technical college," he added. "There is no need to go so far away." I had no choice but to go along with my father's wishes.

From the age of 15, education was no longer free; it was expensive at 150 rubles for six months. Ordinary working people earned only 150 rubles a month. In the Soviet Union, pay was determined by the government's perceived importance of the job you were doing. When I was a technician later on, I would earn 350 rubles a month. An engineer could receive 500 rubles.

Father chose technical college for me. You had to pass an exam to get in. Out of 850, only 150 were accepted for the technical college, and I was one of them. My father was always delighted when I did well. It was a big achievement, a real privilege to get through out of 850 people. He rewarded me with two months in the Black Forest. I had thought I'd like to be a geologist looking for oil and minerals because I liked the country life and it was good to be out in the fresh air. For this course, you had to pass oral and written exams in five subjects. I didn't get high enough marks. Only the top two people got through. My second choice was to be an electromechanical engineer.

In 1940, when I turned 15, I started my first year at technical college, which was specifically designed to produce engineers for industry. It was a big new building, and it was further away than the Russian school. There was a free tram for part of the way, and I had to walk another kilometre from the tram stop. I was scared at first because Donetz was a city with nearly 100,000 people, but I soon got used to it.

When I was at technical college, the trainee doctors from the big clinic would visit to talk to us about the facts of life, diseases, all sorts of things. At the age of 16, you could ask about sex—when to make love and when not to, and so on. Even armed with this knowledge, I didn't do any courting then; that came later.

All day on Saturdays, we had military training. This was serious. We learned how to use grenades and machine guns, how to be snipers, how to drive tanks. Once a year, we put our military skills into practice in a contest between red and blue teams which lasted for a whole week.

In the Soviet Union you were supposedly a free man. In reality, if you opened your mouth out of turn, you could be sent to a Gulag camp, where you'd become a slave and be kept behind barbed wire. You'd probably never get out, and if you didn't work hard enough or produce enough, you didn't eat. The communists needed slaves, and they took a quota for Siberia from each year in school. They continued to send mostly brainy people because they were the ones more likely to cause trouble.

The precariousness of living under communism in the Soviet Union was brought home to us when some of our relatives were sent to Siberia in the late 1920s. My father's sister, Domka, had become separated from her husband because he had been in the White Army and could not return to Ukraine. He lived in Yugoslavia instead. Until 1927, he sent parcels to his wife and children. After that date, Stalin stopped all foreign parcels. Domka's son Alexander attended university in Kiev and became a physics professor. Her daughter Katerina studied foreign languages in Kharkov.

One day, Katerina said something spicy, a joke—I don't know what—and the Chekists grabbed her, her mother, her brother, all three. All the family suffered. Katerina was sent with her mother, Domka, to a prison camp in the peninsula of Kamchatka in the far east of Siberia, for life. The journey was hard, and Domka died on the way. She had been living with us, working in Donetz in the laundry. Luckily for us, the Chekists didn't make the connection between her and my father because she had her husband's surname, not Papucia. Katerina married in Kamchatka and, although I learned her address, I couldn't contact her because she was in exile.

Alexander wasn't sent to Kamchatka, but his passport was stamped *Unwanted* and he was denied work in the Soviet Union.

He had to give up being a physics professor and became a professional artist instead, travelling to wherever he could find work. He was a good artist. He painted scenery in the theatre and also a representation of a folk story on the wall of our bungalow in Kadiyevka. But it was difficult for him to find much of this kind of work. One day, someone was needed to paint a portrait of Lenin, and Alexander had to make a choice—paint for the communists who'd persecuted his family or starve. He painted the portrait, which was then used in the May Day and October parades.

Having done military training at technical college, if I had gone into the army at 18 I would have been a lieutenant straightaway. That was the rule if you had an education. But I just wasn't interested.

I'm glad I wasn't because war was just around the corner.[1]

---

1 Despite their ideological incompatibility, Soviet Russia and Nazi Germany agreed a treaty of mutual non-aggression in August 1939. In September that year, Germany invaded Poland, whereupon Britain and France declared war on Germany, marking the beginning of the Second World War. Then Stalin invaded eastern Poland, and Polish-ruled eastern Galicia and Volhynia with their largely Ukrainian populations were annexed and became united with the rest of Ukraine.

The treaty was violated in June 1941 when Hitler's Nazi Wehrmacht invaded the Soviet Union. The German advance through Ukraine was rapid, and by late 1941, Kiev, Kharkov and Donetsk had fallen. However, towards the end of 1941, the Soviet army began to rally and the Germans were held. Then, with the return of warm weather in the summer of 1942, the Wehrmacht launched a new southeastward offensive towards the Caucasus. However, its Sixth Army failed to capture Stalingrad, was encircled, and surrendered in January 1943. Thereafter the initiative and impetus passed increasingly to the Soviet army, which steadily pressed westward.

The suffering of Ukrainians during the Second World War would be immense. The Russians practised a ruthless scorched earth policy as they retreated, destroying livestock, crops and buildings. Guerrilla groups rampaged behind German lines. Concurrently, Nazi administrators appear to have made little attempt to exploit grievances against the Soviets. Although considerable efforts were made to recruit Ukrainians into the German armed forces, the Nazis continued the collective agricultural policies, massacred Jews, deported ethnic Ukrainians in large numbers to forced labour camps in Germany, and began a programme of depopulation in preparation for German colonisation.

4

THE WINDS OF WAR

In September 1939 Germany invaded Poland, which led to Britain declaring war on Germany. Stalin had signed a non-aggression pact with Hitler and then invaded eastern Poland. Russia also supplied Germany with steel and oil. This meant there was a lot of work for the Russians.

At first, life for us in the Soviet Union continued as normal, but we started to see and feel some of the war's effects. We were close to the border with Poland, a country which Hitler and Stalin had divided up between them. Some 15,000 captured Polish officers are known to have been killed in one Soviet massacre. Many intelligent Polish people like teachers were murdered. There was a railway in Donetsk connecting Ukraine to Siberia. In the winter of 1939/40, I saw about 100 Poles at the station dressed only in thin summer clothing. They shivered pitifully as the armed Chekists surrounded the group with their vicious dogs. I felt so sorry for them. I had heard that thousands of Poles were being sent to Siberia for slave labour, and this was probably the fate of these people.

By early 1941, the situation had changed. I started hearing rumours that the Soviet Union might be attacked by Germany (although it seems that Stalin, surprisingly, discounted this). One afternoon, I returned home from technical college to find my mother crying in the kitchen. On the table was a letter from the authorities.

"Wolodymyr, you've been called up for the quota," she cried, grabbing hold of me and hugging me tightly. "What are we going to do?"

I picked up the letter. It said that I was required to take a rucksack with underwear, soap and food for three days and join a group to be taken east in a few days time. No other information was given. I had been half expecting the call-up as I had turned 16. There were also fewer students at technical college from which to make up Stalin's quota for slave labour. It was still a sickening shock to see it on paper, in black and white.

While my mother wept, a multitude of thoughts ran through my head: Was I going to be a slave in Siberia? Or was I to be drafted into the army ready for war against Germany? Could Father, with his Communist Party connections, do anything to get me excused? All I wanted was to finish my studies, qualify as a technician and have a chance of leading a normal life.

When Father arrived home, he could tell from the redness around my mother's eyes that something was wrong. Without saying anything, she showed him the letter. His face fell as he read it and at first, he could not meet my gaze. "I'm sorry, Wolodymyr, there's nothing I can do," he said. "My connections in the Party are worth nothing. This letter is from the police. You have to go. If you don't, we will all suffer."

I knew that if Father could have had me excused, he would have done. Over the following days, I became resigned to my fate. I had no choice. My mother's weeping continued all night and intermittently over the next two days. She was worried because she knew that many skilled men had been sent to Siberia. I was more concerned that I could be drafted into the army.

On the appointed day, I said a tearful goodbye to my parents and Anna and, with great apprehension, joined the group in Donetsk. My father's last piece of advice rang in my ears: "Keep quiet and do what's asked of you. Try not to draw attention to yourself." By now, this was as easy as breathing.

There were about 40 or 50 of us in the group, all students from the technical college. It was still winter, and we had to march through a heavy snowstorm. The snow was so thick that we couldn't see the road ahead, only the telegraph poles. Dozens of Chekists surrounded us with their rifles. There was no hope of escape. We had no idea where we were going. There was a rumour that we were being taken to the River Volga in an area near Stalingrad. We didn't know if we were being recruited into the army or if we were going to be slaves in Siberia. We were only 16. They could make us do anything.

It wasn't long before I realised I had a problem: I couldn't keep up with the group because I was short of breath, possibly because I was overdressed. "Keep going!" one of the students whispered. I really tried, but we had only walked five or six kilometres from home when I collapsed in the snow. I was so tired, I simply didn't have the strength to continue.

The Chekists could have shot me there and then. I suppose they reasoned that they didn't need to; leaving me behind in sub-zero temperatures would lead to certain death anyway.

I closed my eyes and listened to the sound of the group marching off into the distance. It became quieter and quieter until there was no sound at all. I felt feverishly hot and drifted off to sleep, falling into a lovely dream.

The next thing I knew, someone was shaking me awake. "You're freezing!" It was the voice of a woman aged about 30. She vigorously rubbed my face with ice to wake me up before helping me to stand. Luckily, her house was nearby, and she supported my weight as I hobbled towards it. Without a doubt, this woman saved my life; if she hadn't found me, I would have frozen to death and this story would end here. She set me in front of the fire, wrapped me up in furs and gave me food. I had some left in my rucksack as well.

"You can stay here until you're well enough to leave," said the kind woman. A few days later, I walked home. My mother was overjoyed to see me. It was a miracle. More tears flowed.

Having escaped the clutches of the Chekists, I returned to technical college and resumed my course as if nothing had happened.

In June 1941, notwithstanding Stalin's non-aggression pact with Nazi Germany, Hitler invaded the Soviet Union in a pre-emptive attack code named Operation Barbarossa. Despite the earlier rumours, and also warnings from British intelligence, it seems that Stalin was taken by surprise and the Germans advanced rapidly. Before long they occupied most of Ukraine.

As the Germans approached, the Russians dismantled the factories and the turbines which were generating electricity at the power plant in Kadiyevka. They sent all the skilled people from the power station to the east. Only about five people were left to man it, plus some students who were lucky to remain.

When the war started, the Russians gave every householder a kind of ration card. This entitled the holder to 200 grams of sucher (a dry bread) each day. Sometimes the bread wasn't delivered. Despite this, I never felt desperately hungry. Being a farmer's daughter, my mother was resourceful. She would travel for several days with a little wagon containing clothes and jewellery to the nearest collective farm. The people working there would exchange their food for clothes, and she brought home potatoes and beetroot to fill our bellies and hold off starvation.

In the summer of 1941, I was outside our bungalow near the storage area when, out of nowhere, came a loud, wailing siren. I looked over my shoulder to see the source of this horrible sound—a German Stuka ground-attack aircraft with its Jericho Trumpet heralding its arrival. It was heading directly towards me, and seemed about to attack me. The bungalow was several hundred metres away, and I would never make it back in time. So I started to run for my life towards the storage area which was on stilts. I threw my body to the ground and crawled underneath. I covered my ears and closed my eyes tightly, certain that my time was up, waiting for the blast and the blackness of death.

I waited for an age for the end to come, until eventually I realised that the noise had quietened. The aircraft was flying away. No shots had been fired and no bombs dropped. Perhaps the pilot had just meant to scare me. If so, he had certainly succeeded in his mission.

The Germans reached Donetsk but they did not, in 1941, occupy the area of eastern Ukraine where we lived. They were held up 20 kilometres short of us, largely because of the onset of the harsh, unrelenting winter. We were used to it. The Germans, in contrast, were ill-equipped to deal with such difficult conditions. Snow fell upon snow, and it was so cold that the diesel oil in the Germans' cars froze.

The Germans didn't give up easily and, with the warmer weather of 1942, began pushing forward again. In May, my mother's worst fears came true. My parents received another letter from the Soviet authorities: I was required to join another group heading east. Again, I had to take food for three days.

"My poor Wolodymyr!" cried my mother, weeping uncontrollably. I'd escaped once, it didn't seem likely that I could do so again. My mother became convinced that she'd never see me again and struggled to contain the feelings of panic and fear that were filling her heart.

My father was more positive. "Keep your head down, Wolodymyr, and you'll be all right."

I was not convinced that I would, although I had no choice. Reluctantly, I joined the group on the appointed day. On this second march, there were only about 30 students, all Young Communists. There were about a dozen Russian soldiers guarding us. Again there was no hope of escape. We marched through the Donbas area, and at seven o'clock in the evening we started to climb a hill through a field. Suddenly, some German tanks appeared over the brow of the hill and moved towards us.

Without warning, gun shots rang out. It wasn't the Germans. It was our Russian guards. They were shooting the students on the opposite side of our group. The Russians would rather we died than fall into German hands; our lives were worth nothing. In that split second, I had to make a choice: I could be killed by the Russians or killed by the Germans. I decided to run towards the tanks, along with a boy I knew from technical college. I learned later that we were the only two to escape; all the others, many of them close friends, were shot dead.

The pair of us never looked back. We ran towards the tanks expecting them to fire at any moment.

They didn't. The tanks ignored us and passed us by. It was unbelievable. And as there were no German infantry troops, we just kept running for two or three kilometres, staying in the undergrowth where we could.

Before long I almost tripped over a man lying on the ground. It was a soldier. We looked at him more closely. His uniform was stained with blood, and it was clear that he was dead. We both felt sick with shock, but we carried on running. We ran through more fields littered with dead soldiers, hundreds of them, thousands maybe, Russians and Germans, just lying among the grass and weeds where they'd fallen, unburied. I later learned that, as the Germans advanced, they didn't like to keep prisoners of war because they had to feed them. It was simpler just to shoot them. At first, seeing the dead men horrified and frightened us, but the more we saw, the more we became numb to it, focusing instead on staying alive.

By the evening, we had crept higher up the hill and found thick vegetation which could hide us. Curling up inside our cocoon of plants, shaking with fear and exhaustion, we settled down for the night.

We daren't look for proper shelter. We just wanted to stay out of sight of the Germans. We were terrified they would come near us because we could still hear their tanks. From what we had seen, we knew that they would not think twice about killing us.

At about ten o'clock that evening there was a huge commotion. Soldiers began to march past our hiding place, speaking in Russian. From the snatches of conservation, we could tell that they were retreating. It must have been a whole infantry unit going past us—no horses or cars, just soldiers walking—sometimes just three or four metres away from where we were hiding. I was afraid to move a muscle, scared even to breathe.

In the morning all was silent and we decided to move towards a nearby lake. Later in the day, we looked furtively around and spotted some locals. As they didn't look like a threat to us, we decided to break our cover and headed west until around four in the afternoon. On passing a peasants' cottage, I asked for a drink and they kindly gave us some refreshments. We rested for a while, watching the poultry in the back garden pecking away at some seed.

As we sat there, three German officers, dressed in swimming trunks and jackboots, walked up the hill towards us from the lake. Each had a pistol strapped to his leg. I froze at the sight of their guns, convinced that we were about to be shot.

"You there, give us a chicken," said one in German, looking at me.

"B-but we don't live here," I stammered. My friend cowered next to me.

"Don't be insolent!" the officer shouted. "Give us a bird right now, or we'll take you prisoner."

"I can't," I repeated in desperation. "I have nothing to give you."

They took out their pistols and aimed them at us. "In that case, you're coming with us."

5

CHOOSING SIDES

The German officers (I later learned they were SS) marched us to what they called a Russenlager. This was a prisoner of war camp built specifically for captured Russians. I had no idea that we had been walking so close to it. Like all the Russenlagers, the camp was surrounded by barbed-wire fences and guarded by tanks and watchtowers around the perimeter, manned by machine gunners. The Germans were notorious for treating Russian prisoners of war worse than any other nationality. They saw no need for a hospital, canteen or barracks in a Russenlager.

At the camp, we were greeted by the haunted and miserable faces of thousands of men and boys sitting or lying in the field without any shelter. I'd never seen so many people penned in together in one small place.

Like everyone else, on arrival I was made to take my trousers down so that the Germans could look at my penis. Although it was humiliating, I later realised that my friend and I were lucky. I watched as five men found to be circumcised were frogmarched to the top of a hill, made to stand in a line and then shot in the back—just 150 metres from where I stood. This was the gruesome yet routine fate of anyone brought into the camp who was suspected of being a Jew. They fell dead into a specially dug ditch at the bottom of the hill.

As the men fell down, I was surprised not to feel emotion, but I had seen the Ukrainian students murdered around us on the march and the countless dead soldiers in the fields. At just 17 years old, I was becoming desensitised to death.

Inside the camp, there were no washing facilities. There was no kitchen, no food, no water, nothing. The Russian prisoners were filthy and wore brown uniforms over their terribly thin frames. The stench was overpowering: unwashed bodies mingled with the camp's latrines, which were nothing more than holes in the ground, and the putrid smell of rotting flesh. There were bodies everywhere, just lying where they had breathed their last. This was no prisoner of war camp; it was a death camp.

After a while, a lorry pulled up and the German soldiers threw bread, what seemed to be sardines and water into the mass of prisoners. There was a noisy scramble for the food, and I had no chance to grab anything. These human beings were like a pack of wolves. I still had a little food in my rucksack. I hid it carefully, making sure that no one else would see.

Although it was early summer, the evening was chilly out in the open air. My friend and I had a sleepless night huddled together in the darkness. We were close to the gates and stayed in the same spot.

The following day, at around ten o'clock, I was picked out to be part of a group of about 100 prisoners working outside the camp. I became separated from my friend and would never see him again.

Some of the prisoners were forced to help construct buildings inside the camp. My group had to march fast to a spot about five kilometres away.

When we arrived, we were required to undertake hard labour, using spades to build a road. It was extremely tough work, especially on an almost empty stomach, although I was in better shape than everyone else as I had been in the camp for so little time.

On the second day, I was sitting in my position near the gates inside the death camp when the commandant pulled up in his car. Smartly dressed in his uniform and cap, he was in his fifties and of average height and build. Two soldiers with machine guns accompanied him. As he walked in, he happened to notice me, perhaps because I looked so young.

"Step forward," he said.

I thought he was going to shoot me and shuffled towards him reluctantly.

"How old are you?" he asked, in Ukrainian spoken with a German accent.

"17, sir," I mumbled. What did he want from me? Were these to be the last words I spoke?

"Are you a soldier?"

"No, I'm a student, sir," I said.

"What are you studying?"

"I'm training to become an engineering technician, sir."

"Excellent. What part of Ukraine do you come you from?"

"Near Poltava, sir."

A look of recognition spread across his face. "Ah, Poltava! I was there in the First World War. I know it well."

I smiled tentatively, unsure of what to say next.

The commandant continued. "I have a son just like you. He's a student about the same age."

I nodded.

"Go home, son. You don't belong here."

I was stunned. This mighty commandant was setting me free just because I reminded him of his son back home.[2] If he hadn't spotted and released me, I'm certain that I would have died in this camp like the thousands of Russian soldiers whose bodies had just been left to rot.

Luckily, I wasn't far away from home, now under German occupation. I could and did walk there in a few hours. When I got back, Mother and Anna greeted me enthusiastically. Father wasn't there.

"Where is Father?" I asked.

Mother shook her head sorrowfully. "He's been taken away. He's a prisoner of war too."

Just after I'd gone on the march, the Germans had carried out a random check. They'd picked up my father in the street and taken him to a civilian prisoner of war camp. In his absence, my mother had to sell everything she owned in order to buy food. With no idea where Father was being held, I didn't know what to do. It was the start of an anxious wait.

Much to my mother's relief, he came home in the third week, looking thinner and drawn. It was

---

2 *That decision by the commandant was probably less whimsical than it seemed to Wolodymyr at the time. In late 1941, the Nazi authorities had issued a directive allowing the release of Ukrainians, Balts or Belorussians from the camps if a relative claimed them or if there were some other plausible reason. Evidently, they regarded these nationalities as less of a threat, or possibly more human, than Russians. However, the Nazis soon changed their minds, and rescinded that concession.*

the second time in his life that he had been a prisoner of war. The first was in the Russian Civil War when he was a Morse code operator working for the White Army at their headquarters in the Caucasus area of Ukraine. He'd been taken captive by the Bolsheviks and forced to work for the Red Army on the southern front. People like my father who could communicate using Morse code were scarce. The only reason he wasn't killed then was because he was such a valuable asset with his communication skills.

With this earlier experience, perhaps he had known how to play it in the German camp, keeping his cool until the opportunity arose to escape. Prisoners there had been encouraged to join the German army. Many Ukrainians had already enlisted in the Wehrmacht, and my father volunteered also. After a few days, he saw a chance, removed his uniform and ran. There was no way the Germans could trace him because they had never asked for his address.

The German authorities reinstated my father in his old job at the power plant. Unfortunately, by then the technical college had closed, and I was not able to continue with my course. Luckily, my father found me work at the power station as an instrument technician in the laboratory. I was paid 350 rubles a month, and I enjoyed the work. I would have liked to have been an electromechanical engineer in a power station for the rest of my life. But everything changed because of the war. By August 1942 all my friends had disappeared. It was difficult to keep in touch with anyone, and nobody was making plans.

At that time, the only people keeping the power plant going with the couple of turbines left were retired people and a handful of students like me who had managed to survive. The Russian partisans had tried to sabotage the power plant and burn it down because it was under German control. I was asked to prepare a detailed technical drawing of the distances between the bolts where the old turbines had once been. This would enable the Germans to build or bring in new turbines.

Father worked from the summer until New Year 1943. Then he suddenly became ill. It was his old stomach problems but this time it was different. It was much worse. We knew that he would not survive.

"Wolodymyr, please put a cross on my grave," he said one day. Religion was banned under communism, but Father still had faith inside him.

"Yes, Father," I said.

The tide of war had now definitely turned against the Wehrmacht. At the end of 1943, Stalingrad was finally liberated. The Russian army was advancing and we could now hear the heavy thud of mortars firing at all hours of the day. I knew that if the Russians came back, they would kill me because I had escaped from them twice already. We also had very little money coming in because of Father's illness, only my small wage from the power plant.

We had received letters from my Uncle Pavlo, the priest, who incredibly had somehow escaped from Siberia. For a while, he'd settled in Kharkov and worked for a rich communist there as a gardener while his wife was a cook. (He could not, of course, be a priest again under communism.) He had then, in 1941, returned to Falenko, my birthplace. As this was the area of Ukraine under German occupation, he had managed to get his property back.

During Father's last days, I discussed the situation with my mother: "If we head back to Falenko, we'll be under German control," I said. "We'll be much safer." Choosing the right side was vital to ensure we survived the war. I instinctively knew that living under German occupation, although hazardous, would give us a better chance.

Reluctantly, my mother agreed. "Perhaps you can find work there," she said hopefully.

Father died on 1 February 1943, leaving my mother heartbroken. We had accepted that he was seriously ill, although his death was probably largely from a lack of medical care. He was just under 50. Some carpenters he had known built a coffin, and we buried him in the local cemetery on 2 February. It was just my mother and me at the funeral.

I was never able to carry out Father's request to put a cross on his grave. The day after we buried him, we ran away. We left everything: the bungalow, the painting my cousin Alexander had done, our papers. For the second time in my life, my mother, Anna and I were fleeing in secrecy just to survive. With Father gone, I was responsible for my family. I needed to provide for them, and I knew that was no longer possible in Kadiyevka.

We headed west, back towards Falenko, some 300 kilometres away (Map 3).[3] First, however, we would walk to nearby Horlivka, where our relative Schevchenko lived. We hoped that he could give us useful advice and help. However, when we reached his house, the door was answered by a frail old lady—Schevchenko's 90-year-old mother. "He's not here," she said. "He left three days ago heading west." Like us, Schevchenko had decided to keep ahead of the advancing Russians. Clearly there was nothing for us in Horlivka. We would also have to continue travelling west.

---

3 *The sketch map shows a straight line connecting their place of departure with their destination. The actual route they took cannot now be determined, but it was not as direct as this. Their course deviated widely as they proceeded.*

It was the middle of winter and the snow lay two or three metres deep. With no horses, all we could do was plod along on foot, pulling our sledge behind us. With no map or compass, only a handful of possessions and a small amount of money, we started walking. I followed the sun from east to west and used my fairly sparse knowledge of topography to get my bearings.

Dressed in furs, valenki and waxed animal-skin gloves, my mother and I took turns to pull the sledge while Anna, who was only 14, walked alongside. I was the man of the family, but it was my mother who had the mental toughness needed to keep going in the appalling conditions.

At times the temperature fell to minus 20˚C—dangerously cold. If we stopped moving for too long, we could succumb to hypothermia. We walked from early morning until five or six in the evening. By the afternoons we started looking out for a house, somewhere we could stay the night. If we didn't have shelter overnight we knew that we could easily die, making it vitally important to find somewhere before darkness fell.

Houses were few and far between in the Ukrainian countryside. The Ukrainian people that we met, though, always gave us a warm welcome. They could see that we were poor and hungry, and took pity on us, offering us food—usually a little

Wally aged 14/15 years in 1939/40, when he was
a member of the Young Communist Party

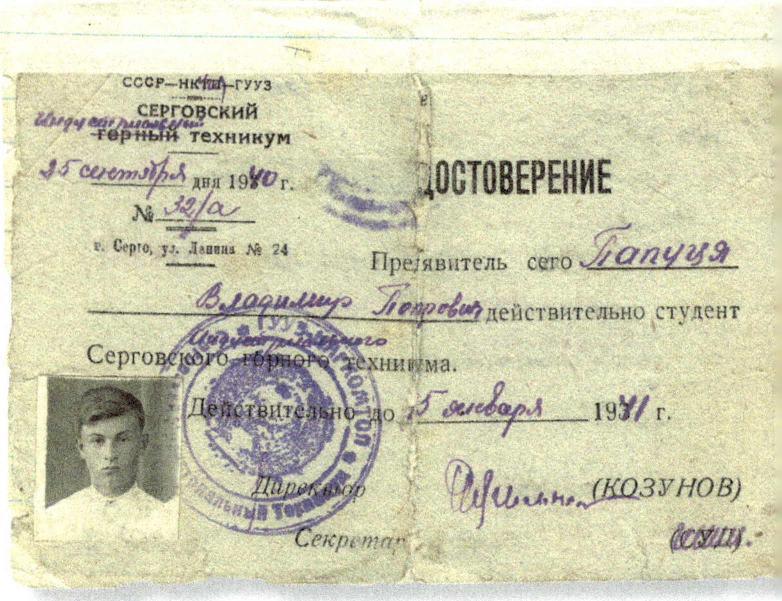

СССР—НК...—ГУУЗ
СЕРГОВСКИЙ
горный техникум
25 сентября дня 1940 г.
№ 32/а
г. Серго, ул. Ленина № 24

...ДОСТОВЕРЕНИЕ

Предъявитель сего Папуця
Владимир Петрович действительно студент
Серговского горного техникума.
Действительно до 15 января 1941 г.
Директор (КОЗУНОВ)
Секретар...

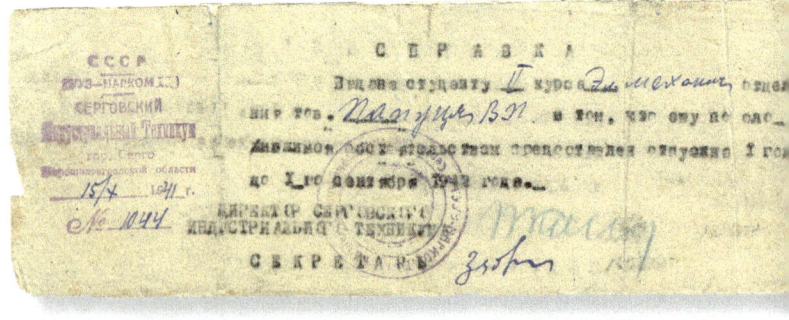

Russian ID document dated 1940 showing that 15-year-old Wally was a Russian student. If the Germans had found this document, they would have killed him

СССР
ГУУЗ—НАРКОМ...
СЕРГОВСКИЙ
Индустриальный Техникум
гор. Серго
Ворошиловградской области
15/IV 1941 г.
№ 1044

СПРАВКА

Выдана студенту II курса Эл. механич. отделения тов. Папуця В.П. в том, что ему ... предоставлен отпуск ... до 1-го сентября 1941 года.

ДИРЕКТОР СЕРГОВСКОГО ИНДУСТРИАЛЬНОГО ТЕХНИКУМА
СЕКРЕТАРЬ

CCCP (Soviet) document dated 15 April 1941. Electrical technician's certificate written in Russian. This states that Wally has passed the course & has permission to start the next electrical technician's course

Russian school report dated 1940, when Wally was aged 15.
N = Satisfactory, X = Very good, 0 = Excellent

An improvised camp for Soviet prisoners of war, August 1942

Bread being distributed to prisoners
in a Russenlager, July 1941

German ID photo.
Ellwangen 1944.
Wally was 19

Wally aged 20,
Germany, 1945

Wally's mother, Maria, aged 40. Germany, 1945

Bescheinigung

Papuca Waldemar

Wir bescheinigen den ....
geb. am 28.3.25 .... wohnh. in H.-Sontheim ....
dass er in unseren Werk seit... 25.6.45 .. beschäftigt ist.

Heilbronn, den 27.Juni 45 Elektrizitätswerk Heilbronn a. N.

i.A. Müller

ID document, dated 25 June 1945, stating that Wally is Polish
& born in Sontheim. This is the document he managed
to obtain from the Polish consulate

CERTIFICATE

Basing on authentical informations we state that

Mr. (Mrs. Miss) Wolodymyr
         P a p u c i a

calling electrician

born the 28.3.1925.

in Wolodymyr wol. Poland,

now living in Augsburg

is Ukrainian.

Augsburg, 194 5

Secretary: Chairman:

Wolodymyr Papucia
Signature of holder

Remarks:

Mr. Wolodymyr Papucia has declared to be stateless,

UKRAINIAN SERVICE
for Counsel and Aid

in Augsburg

No 645/3

A Ukrainian Service for Counsel and Aid in
Augsburg document, June 1945. This shows
that Wally is an electrician

Der Bürgermeister
der Gemeinde Untergruppenbach
Kreis Heilbronn
Girokonto Nr. 24 Kreissparkasse Heilbronn

Untergruppenbach, ben 18. Dezember 1945.

Bescheinigung.

Dem Waldemar P a p u c a, geb. 28.März 1925, wird hiermit
bescheinigt, daß er hier wohnhaft ist und im Wald als Waldarbeiter
(Holzeinschlag) beschäftigt ist.

German document dated 18 December 1945. This states
that Wally worked in the forest. Wally could have used this as
proof that he was a lumberjack/tree specialist
in order to move to Canada

Freiw. Feuerwehr
Heilbronn

Heilbronn (Neckar), den 22. Oktober 1946
Wilhelmstr. 27 - Eingang Südstr.
Fernsprecher Nr. 48/25, App. 88

Herrn Waldemar Papuca geb. am 28.3.1925 wird bestätigt, dass
Er bis Mai 1945 Angehöriger der Feuerwehr Heilbronn war.

Freiwillige Feuerwehr
Heilbronn
J. A.

Document dated 22 October 1946 stating that Wally had
been a fireman in the city of Heilbronn

76

Wally aged 21, Germany 1946

Meldekarte
für den Bezug der Lebensmittelkarten

Name: Papuca

Vorname: Waldemar (bei Frauen auch Geburtsname)

Geburtstag: 28.3.1925   Familienstand: ledig
(led., verh., verw., gesch.)

Wohnort: Untergruppenbach

Straße: Turnhalle   Nr.:

Erlernter Beruf: Elektro-Monteur

Zur Zeit beschäftigt als (bei Selbständigen auch Art des Gewerbebetriebs
usw.) Arbeiter

(z. B. selbständiger Bäcker, Mithilfe in elterl. Landwirtschaft, Hausfrau,
Schüler usw.)

(Eigenhändige Unterschrift des Inhabers)

Diese Meldekarte ist vor jeder Lebensmittelkarten-Ausgabe **auf der Rückseite** mit einem **Bestätigungsvermerk** versehen zu lassen und zwar:
1. Für in Beschäftigung stehende Arbeiter, Angestellte, Lehrlinge, sowie Beamte **durch den Arbeitgeber oder Behördenvorstand**
2. Für Selbständige aller Art, mithelfende Familienangehörige, sowie Hausfrauen, Rentner und sonstige Nichtbeschäftigte **durch das Arbeitsamt**
3. Für Kranke **durch die Krankenkasse**
4. Für Schüler und Studenten **durch die Schulbehörde**
5. Für Meldepflichtige zu Ziffer 2 und 3, an deren Wohnort sich kein Arbeitsamt oder Krankenkasse befindet, **durch das Bürgermeisteramt.**

Mißbrauch wird bestraft!

(Vermerke des Arbeitsamts)

Berufsgruppe und -Art:

Abgleichung AK:

(Dienststempel des Arbeitsamts)

I. 46 / 541

This page & next: German food card, dated 1946. You had to show you were working in order to receive food & a stamp on the card. The card shows Wally as an electrician

78

Achtung! Der **Arbeitgeber** bestätigt durch nachstehenden Eintrag, daß der Meldekarteninhaber bei ihm in Arbeit steht. Für „Gelegenheitsarbeit" oder kurzfristige Tätigkeit darf kein Bestätigungsvermerk gegeben werden. **Mißbrauch und falsche Angaben werden bestraft!**

Bestätigungsvermerke mit Stempel, Datum und Unterschrift versehen!

87. Periode ab 1. 4. 1946.	1. April 1946
Bestätigungsvermerk	Stempel der Lebens-mittelkartenausgabestelle
88. Periode ab 29. 4. 1946.	
Bestätigungsvermerk	Stempel der Lebens-mittelkartenausgabestelle
89. Periode ab 27. 5. 1946.	
Bestätigungsvermerk	Stempel der Lebens-mittelkartenausgabestelle
90. Periode ab 24. 6. 1946.	
Bestätigungsvermerk	Stempel der Lebens-mittelkartenausgabestelle
91. Periode ab 22. 7. 1946.	
Bestätigungsvermerk	Stempel der Lebens-mittelkartenausgabestelle
92. Periode ab 19. 8. 1946.	
Bestätigungsvermerk	Stempel der Lebens-mittelkartenausgabestelle
93. Periode ab 16. 9. 1946.	
Bestätigungsvermerk	Stempel der Lebens-mittelkartenausgabestelle
94. Periode ab 14. 10. 1946.	
Bestätigungsvermerk	Stempel der Lebens-mittelkartenausgabestelle

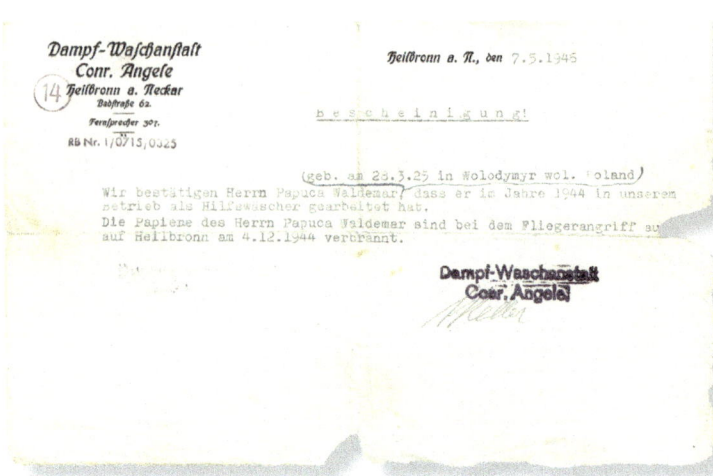

German document dated 7 May 1946 stating that Wally
works in a laundry & is unskilled. He kept this in case
he was picked up by the Russians

Wally with classmates at the UNESCO camp. His great friend
Ivan is second from right, next to Wally, far right

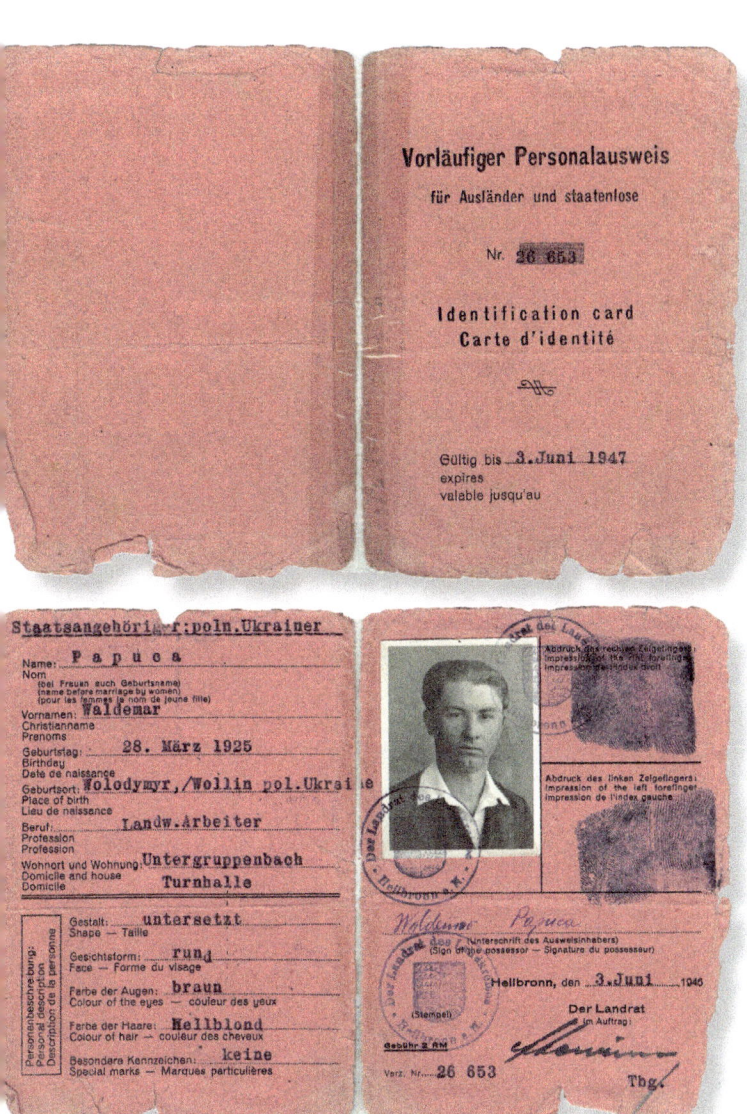

Vorläufiger Personalausweis

für Ausländer und staatenlose

Nr. 26 653

Identification card
Carte d'identité

Gültig bis 3. Juni 1947
expires
valable jusqu'au

Staatsangehöriger:poln.Ukrainer

Name: **Papuca**
Nom
(bei Frauen auch Geburtsname)
(name before marriage by women)
(pour les femmes le nom de jeune fille)

Vornamen: **Waldemar**
Christianname
Prénoms

Geburtstag: **28. März 1925**
Birthday
Date de naissance

Geburtsort: **Wolodymyr,/Wollin pol.Ukraine**
Place of birth
Lieu de naissance

Beruf: **Landw.Arbeiter**
Profession
Profession

Wohnort und Wohnung **Untergruppenbach**
Domicile and house
Domicile **Turnhalle**

Gestalt: **untersetzt**
Shape — Taille

Gesichtsform: **rund**
Face — Forme du visage

Farbe der Augen: **braun**
Colour of the eyes — couleur des yeux

Farbe der Haare: **Hellblond**
Colour of hair — couleur des cheveux

Besondere Kennzeichen: **keine**
Special marks — Marques particulières

Abdruck des rechten Zeigefingers:
Impression of the right forefinger
Impression de l'index droit

Abdruck des linken Zeigefingers:
Impression of the left forefinger
Impression de l'index gauche

(Unterschrift des Ausweisinhabers)
(Sign of the possessor — Signature du possesseur)

Hellbronn, den 3. Juni 1946

Der Landrat
im Auftrag:

(Stempel)

Gebühr 2 RM

Verz. Nr. 26 653

Tbg.

German ID document dated 3 June 1946. It states
that Wally is from the Polish part of Ukraine and
has brown eyes & blond hair

81

1946 UNESCO camp. Wally is seated on the far left.
Ivan is standing, second from right

While in the UNESCO camp in 1946, Wally and his friends went to a camp for young people. Wally is kneeling

Ukrainian Gymnasium (Grammar School) in *Ellvangen (Jagst) Württemb.*

Num. *2*

HALFYEARLY CERTIFICATE

Papucia Walodymyr,

born on *the 28 of March* 19*26* scholar of the *seven* class,

obtains the following certificate for the school halfyear 194*6*/4*7*

Conduct	*very good*
Religion	*good*
Ukrainian	*good*
Latin	*sufficient*
English	*sufficient*
German	*sufficient*
History	*good*
Geography	*good*
Natural History	*very good*
Chemistry	*very good*
Physics	*very good*
Mathematics	*good*
Descriptive Geometry	
Philosophy	
Drawing	*very good*
Singing	
Physical Training	*very good*

General Progress:

Omitted *15* hours

of them non excused

Ellvangen the 31 of December 194*6*

Director.

Class Master.

Conduct: 1 very good, 2 good, 3 passable, 4 unpassable.
Progress: 1 very good, 2 good, 3 sufficient, 4 insufficient

A school report dated December 1946 in Russian & English
from the Ukrainian Gymnasium

84

The young people's camp, 1946

Wally (sixth from right) looking thin
at the UNESCO camp in 1946

Medical certificate dated 6 August 1947 from
Ulm hospital (PCIRO section) in Bavaria

Medical clearance document issued in 1947

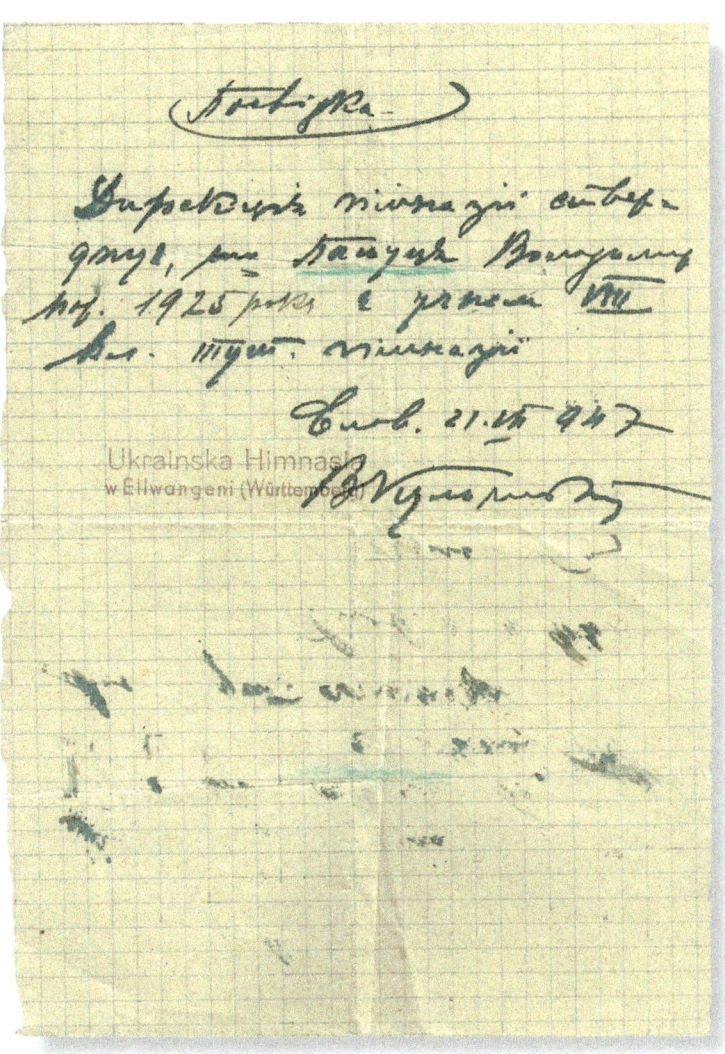

Handwritten note dated 21 July 1947 in black ink from the UNESCO school, stating that Wally has completed his studies & is eligible/supported to go to university

US2S/M - 2/24.

Office of the Military Governor № 116007

U. S. Zone of Germany

CERTIFICATE OF IDENTITY IN LIEU OF PASSPORT

116007

1. .... P A P U C A .... Wolodymyr ....
(name in full)

born at ....Saluszje......, ...Wolodimir Wolynsk..., ...Poland....
(town)   (district)   (country)

on ...28.... of ...March...., ...1925...., ...M...., ...Polimin....
(day)   (month)   (year)   (sex)   (citizenship)

.... intends to emigrate to

(given & maiden name of wife, if applicable)

....
(country of [t]ms [n]ation)

2. He (she) will be accompanied by .....none.....

(List here all family members, with
name, birthplace and date, and
citizenship of each)

....

....

3. His (her) occupation is ...Factory worker...

4. DESCRIPTION

Height .....5.... ft ....8.... inches

Hair ...blond... Eyes ....brown....

Distinguishing marks or features:

.... Wolodymyr
(signature of applicant)

5. He (she) solemnly declares that he (she) has never committed nor has he (she) been convicted of any crime except as follows: ....

6. He (she) is unable to produce birth certificates, marriage license, divorce papers and / or police record for the following reasons: ....

7. I hereby certify that the description of the person(s) whose photograph(s) is affixed hereto is correct and that he (she, they) declare(s) that the facts stated above are true.

Papuca Wolodymyr
(signature of applicant)

Signed ...., ...Dec., ...1947....
(day)   (month)   (year)

at ...Stuttgart...
(location)

Paul J McConnell
(signature of certifying officer)

....
(position)

December 1947. Original certificate of identity in
lieu of a passport. Issued by the repatriation
& resettlement office in Stuttgart

Ukrainian Gymnasium
at Ellwangen/Jagst/
Germany.

Ellwangen

the 26th Aprile, 1948.

CERTIFICATE.

This is to certify that PAHUCA Wolodymyr, Religion orthodox, nation. Ukrainian, born on the 28th March, 1925 was a pupil of the 8th class of Ukrainian Gymnasium at Ellwangen until 25th November, 1947 and left for England.

As a pupil he was diligent and good succeeded.

Director of Ukrainian
Gymnasium at Ellwangen.

Certificate issued by the director of the school at the
UNESCO camp in 1948, stating that Wally
was a successful pupil

Top: with Uncle Andre Papuca in the late 1940s at
Brockhurst camp outside Gloucester
Bottom: Frome agricultural workers' camp, 1948.
Wally far right with two other Ukrainians, names unknown

Ukrainian agricultural workers' camp, Frome, 1948. Wally
was living with others in one of 12 Nissen huts

Membership card dated 11 November 1948 stating
that Wally is a member of the Association of
Ukrainians in Great Britain Ltd

Wally enjoying a day off from one of the farms he
worked on in Frome, 1948. Notice the hayrick

1949. Wally, right, working as an orderly at
Combe Down Isolation Hospital, Bath

Bath to Weymouth train, 1952

Weymouth, 1953

Burnham-on-Sea, 1953

WESTLAND AIRCRAFT LIMITED

YEOVIL
ENGLAND

TELEPHONE
YEOVIL   1100

OUR REF   WP/TL/GC/2,0.1.

YOUR REF

TELEGRAMS
AIRCRAFT   YEOVIL

28th November, 1955.

W. Papuca, Esq.,
24, Southdown Avenue,
BATH,
Somerset.

Dear Sir,

We have pleasure in returning herewith Certificate of Naturalization No. BNA.32752.

This has been found to be in order, and we look forward to your commencing here on Monday, the 5th December, 1955.

Yours faithfully,
for WESTLAND AIRCRAFT LIMITED,

J.H. Lacey.

pp   Personnel Officer.

Telegram from Westland Aircraft on 28 November 1955
offering Wally a position as an engineer

Post Office Money Orders, Postal Orders or Cheques should be made payable to the Accounting Officer, Home Office, and crossed "Bank of England, Account Paymaster General". Bank of England notes should not be sent by Post.

The Certificate will be sent to you as soon as possible after receipt of the fee and the completed forms, but if there is delay in the payment of the fee and the submission of the forms, you may be required to comply with further conditions before the Certificate is issued.

~~Children.~~ ~~There are enclosed letter (A.P.46.H)~~

I am, **Sir,**
Your obedient Servant,

I am to explain that it is not possible to show your nationality as Ukrainian because there is no Ukrainian state recognised by Her Majesty's Government as exercising sovereignty over your birthplace. The Secretary of State proposes, therefore, to show your nationality and that of your parents as Polish.

Mr. W. Papuca,
24, Southdown Avenue,
Bath,
Somerset.

N 276/53

Document dated 17 July 1954 from the Secretary of State.
This states that the Ukrainian state is not recognised
by the British government and Wally's nationality
is to be shown as Polish

Certificate No. **BNA** 32752   Home Office No. F. 52358.

BRITISH NATIONALITY ACT, 1948.

CERTIFICATE OF NATURALISATION

Whereas   Wolodymyr Papuca

has applied to one of Her Majesty's Principal Secretaries of State for a certificate of naturalisation, alleging with respect to   him self the particulars set out below, and has satisfied the Secretary of State that the conditions laid down in the British Nationality Act, 1948, for the grant of a certificate of naturalisation are fulfilled :

Now, therefore, the Secretary of State, in pursuance of the powers conferred upon him by the said Act, grants to the said

Wolodymyr Papuca

this Certificate of Naturalisation, and declares that upon taking the Oath of Allegiance within the time and in the manner required by the regulations made in that behalf he   shall be a citizen of the United Kingdom and Colonies as from the date of this certificate.

In witness whereof I have hereto subscribed my name this   30. day of
July , 19 54

HOME OFFICE.   J. aNewJam
LONDON.   UNDER SECRETARY OF STATE.

PARTICULARS RELATING TO APPLICANT.

Full Name	Wolodymyr PAPUCA.
Address	24, Southdown Avenue, Bath, Somerset.
Profession or Occupation	Ward Orderly.
Place and date of birth	Saluszje, Poland. 28th March, 1925.
Nationality	Polish.
Single, married, etc.	Single.
Name of wife or husband	- - -
Names and nationalities of parents	Petro and Maria PAPUCA (Polish).

(For Oath
see overleaf.)

This page and next: Certificate of Naturalisation, 30 July 1954

102

Oath of Allegiance

I, *Wolodymyr Papuca*

swear by Almighty God that I will be faithful and bear true allegiance to Her Majesty, Queen Elizabeth the Second, Her Heirs and Successors, according to law.

(Signature) *W. Papuca*

Sworn and subscribed this *16th* day of *August* 19*54*, before me,

(Signature)

~~Justice of the Peace for~~
A Commissioner for Oaths.

Name and Address
(in Block Capitals)
G. A. BURNINGHAM,
5, PIERREPONT ST. BATH

Unless otherwise indicated hereon, if the Oath of Allegiance is not taken within one calendar month of the date of this Certificate, the Certificate shall have no effect.

HOME OFFICE
- 2 SEP 1954
REGISTERED

Wally, 1958, Clevedon

Wally aged 83 years, taken in 2008

Wally with his six grandchildren & his son Nick

dry bread, beetroot and potatoes. Occasionally, we were given pieces of salted pork or salami or some spiced apples. This was the only meal we ate each day. To stave off thirst, we drank melted snow. After we had eaten, the homeowners would usually allow us to take shelter for the night. Often we slept on the floor in a line next to the people who lived there. Along the way, we exchanged Mother and Father's best clothes for food, whatever we could get. We were determined to stay alive.

The people in whose homes we stayed pointed us in the right direction. Telegraph poles also helped us to find our way through the snowy landscape. We could only travel about 20 kilometres a day, dragging our weary bodies through the freezing air, willing our feet to take another painful step over the snowy ground. All the while there was the sound of guns and mortars in the distance, keeping our nerves on edge. Occasionally, we heard a lonely wolf call out although we never saw one. Nor did we see many people. It was just too cold to be outside.

We walked every day, never taking a break. Our bellies ached through lack of food and our whole bodies were sore. Through exhaustion and hunger, we kept going. With the rope over my shoulder, I pulled the sledge on and on through fields and fields of snow. When we came to a hill, my mother or I would take the rope, face the sledge and pull it up the slope using all the strength we had. Whoever wasn't pulling stood behind the sledge and pushed.

After walking for about two months, we finally reached our destination—Falenko, the village where I was born—feeling overwhelmed by relief that our journey was over. I saw again the familiar buildings of my early childhood. By the time we reached our village, the snow had started to melt.

We must have smelt awful—we had not changed our clothes for the last two months—and we looked like skeletons by the time we arrived. Uncle Pavlo and his wife took us in. We rested our weary bones and enjoyed the comfortable familiarity of being in the home of a relative. After a while Uncle Pavlo started to encourage us to try to get our own house back.

"The Germans will help you," he said.

I tried hard to do this. Unfortunately, part of our farmhouse had been turned into a barn for pigs and cows. There was a family of communists living there too, which meant that we only regained half of the house. I was upset about it because the Germans didn't want to get involved and wouldn't allow me to get rid of the Russian who had the other half (I would have killed him if I could).

There were three families living in the big house where Uncle Konstantin had lived. He had not returned.

It was the spring of 1943.[4] In Falenko there were no young people. Indeed, almost everyone between the ages of 16 and 60 had gone, the men

---

4 In 1943 the Second World War swung decisively against Germany. The USA was now also an adversary. Germany was being subjected to continual aerial bombardment by the British air force by night and the American air force by day. In June 1944, Anglo-American armies landed in Normandy and advanced eastwards. Southern Germany, where the present narrative is now focussed, lay in the American sector of operations. Meanwhile, the Soviet army continued relentlessly west. Hitler shot himself on 30 April 1945. Berlin fell to the Russians on 2 May. The Second World War in Europe ended six days later.

The numbers of ethnic Ukrainians who had fought in the Soviet army are thought to be between 4.5 and 7 million. Of the estimated 8.7 million Soviet troops who fell in battle in that war, some 1.4 million were Ukrainians. Pro-Soviet partisans operating in Ukraine are further estimated at around 50,000 in 1941, increasing to 500,000 in 1944, about half of these being ethnic Ukrainians.

Other Ukrainians, under various designations, had fought alongside the Nazis. Estimates of their numbers range from 15,000 to 100,000.

Additionally, huge numbers of Ukrainians, perhaps as many as a million, had been deported to work in Germany.

The total losses inflicted on the Ukrainian population during the Second World War are believed to be between 5 and 8 million.

Stalin's paranoia, always prominent, became exacerbated and he became increasingly unstable post-war. Ever fearful of treachery, he ordered the deportation or execution of any Soviet citizens suspected of wartime subversion. Even those, often indeed especially those, who had been imprisoned or subjected to forced labour by Germany, were endangered.

conscripted into the German army, the women forced to work. Many of the latter had been deported to Germany. Anyone who was left was working on collective farms. At almost 18, I was the youngest adult by many years. It was a strange feeling living in a place with no other people my age. And everyone was jealous because I'd managed to survive unlike so many others.

My mother's brother, Nicholas, was in the Ukrainian police as deputy commandant in a town called Chutove, about 25 kilometres from Falenko (Map 2). I had not been able to find any work. Then Nicholas said he could give me a job in the police station. I joined the police because I really didn't want to go to Germany. I was happy to be back in Falenko and wanted to stay. I was given an old Russian rifle and ammunition, but I had no uniform, just civilian clothes with a white band on my arm. I was one of only 13 policemen in Falenko, and we had to look after about six villages.

As part of the Ukrainian police, we were, of course, working for the German occupiers. Our role involved arresting smugglers, fighting Russian partisans and dealing with any complaints or unrest. I arrested one or two people in the four months I spent as a policeman. One was a deserter from the Russian army working in one of the villages. In my opinion, he hadn't done anything wrong but people had complained about him. I know I shouldn't have done it, but I was afraid of him because he was bigger than me. I took him to the headquarters. I didn't know what else to do with him. I don't know what happened to him after that.

During the war, fighting had disturbed the natural habitat of the local wolves. Normally wary of humans, the packs now started to come through the village, trying to attack the horses. All 13 of us policemen tried to find and shoot the wolves. However, wolves have excellent hearing and sense of smell, and they always escaped.

At night, the police had to guard the village council building where the guns were kept; there had been a spate of thefts after dark. A chap who was on night duty got into trouble because he was asleep on the job. One night, he was fully awake when he heard a voice. "Who's there?" he called out. There was no reply, but then there was movement again. He fired his gun and shot a man right in the head. It was the chief of police, stealing the guns.

A German counter attack had forced some Russian soldiers into a marshy, boggy area. I was sent west in that direction, about 15 kilometres from Falenko, to check out what was going on. I didn't know the area, and when I arrived, I saw a group of about 15 women hoeing. "Go, go, go!" they whispered urgently to me. I realised that I was headed straight for where the Russian troops were hiding, just behind the next hill. Again, my life was spared.

The Russians frequently dropped partisans into the area by parachute while I was in the police. Their job was to carry out daring acts of sabotage, as well as to glean information from the locals. I was often sent to different areas to try to locate the partisans. Luckily, I never came face to face with one.

By late 1943, the main Russian forces were getting so close that we could hear them advancing. In some areas around us, the Germans had started to retreat. The German commandant in charge of our village told us to leave before the Russians arrived.

"You've been working for us," he said. "If the Russians find you, they'll kill you. Leave now while you can."

We didn't need to be told twice.

6

ESCAPE THROUGH
THE WAR ZONE

I was only 18, and the responsibility of looking after my mother and sister weighed heavily on me. Before we could escape Falenko, we needed two horses and a cart. None of us could bear the thought of making another epic journey on foot. And in any case, the Russians were approaching fast. I took the initiative and walked to the nearest collective farm with my mother and sister. I was still wearing my policeman's armband, and I was armed with a gun. The farmer came out and walked towards me. I aimed at him. "We need two of your horses and a cart. Now."

He just stood there and looked me up and down dismissively. "Why should I give you our animals?"

My youth was clearly a disadvantage. I had to be more assertive. "Two horses and a cart," I repeated in a louder voice, and cocked the gun.

Now the farmer could see I meant business. I had about 40 bullets and I wasn't afraid to use them. Without another word, he opened the stable door, led the horses out and harnessed them to the cart.

Getting those horses and the cart was a matter of life and death. If the farmer hadn't relented, I would have shot him. Before he could change his mind, my mother jumped up on to the cart followed by Anna and me. Mother drove it out of the yard as fast as she could while I looked behind, still pointing my gun at the farmer.

My mother was still an expert at driving horses, and she would become our saviour in the chaotic days ahead. We travelled to Chutove to link up with her brother, the deputy police commandant, plus the 12 other policemen and their families. The journey was extremely risky because we were heading towards the area where we knew the Russians were fighting. We figured there would be safety in numbers if we joined up with the other police.

On our way to Chutove, we passed through countless burning, deserted villages. All was in flames and acrid smoke hung in the air. Every building had been destroyed by the Germans as they retreated. I could understand why they'd done it: before we left our place in Falenko, I had asked the Germans to burn down our farm too. I would rather see it destroyed than fall into Russian hands again.

However, on reaching Chutove, we discovered that the chief of police and my mother's brother had fled three days earlier. We'd risked our lives going east for nothing. All we could do was try to catch up with the other policemen and their families by continuing to travel west, straight through the war zone.

Day and night, there was the continuous crackle of gunfire and the boom of shells. It sounded as if the Russians were both in front of and behind us. In fact, we were just about five kilometres ahead of the Russian battle line. We never felt safe. Twice we were close to a Russian advance party. From a distance, they looked at us and we looked at them. There were no more than a dozen of us with our families, and probably about 50 of them. As we weren't a threat to them, nothing happened.

It was only down to the skill of my mother driving the horses that we made it out of the war zone safely. We were all exhausted, having only had a few hours' sleep between us. Whenever we needed provisions, we exchanged clothes for food.

It took several days to reach the huge bridge at the River Dnieper north of Kiev (Map 1). We had now travelled some 350 kilometres from Falenko. As we arrived, there was bad news. The retreating

Germans had troops guarding the bridge. A German officer walked towards us to stop us going any further.

"You can't cross here," he said firmly. "It's a target for the Russian planes, so it's not safe. The roads are only for soldiers, not civilians."

"But we have to get to the other side," I said.

He shook his head and waved us away from the bridge. We stood together as a group, wondering what to do next.

My mother was undeterred, pointing down the road. "Let's go further that way and find a shallow place to cross."

By now, Mother's skill in driving the horses was legendary, and everyone was happy to follow her lead. We continued on for about a kilometre before we found a spot that was shallow enough. My mother drove her cart across first to show that the horses could cross safely there. The others followed, taking the same route. The Russians were shelling the whole area, and we all felt happier once we had safely crossed the river.

On the other side, we joined up with some other former members of the Ukrainian police, including the ones we'd missed in Chutove. Mother was relieved to see her brother and his family again. Altogether, there were now about 300 of us. The Germans directed us to the city of Vinnitsia, another 350 kilometres southwest towards the Polish border

(Map 1). They told us to leave our horses and take only what we could carry. We faced another long, laborious trek, although it was less dangerous.

Vinnitsia was chaotic, with hundreds of people there all trying to flee the Russians. By now, several other groups had joined ours, making about 1,000 of us in total. We were directed to cars in a long goods train that was destined for Krakow in Poland, about 700 kilometres away. We had no idea why we were going there, but as we had been part of the police force who had worked for the Germans we felt safe. The journey took three days, and the train regularly stopped at the stations along the route, enabling us to get food and drink.

When we reached Krakow, we had to wait two or three days in shelters in an internment camp. It was a big assembly centre with hundreds of people behind barbed wire, guarded by the Germans. After three days there, we were put on to another goods train with about 60 cars. Still we were not given any information. There were no proper seats because it wasn't a passenger train. More worryingly, our guns had been taken away. There was no point in fearing the future, I reasoned. By then I was used to uncertainty.

We eventually arrived at Stuttgart in Germany. Straightaway, we were ushered into a large hall where row upon row of Germans sat behind tables. They were civilians, not soldiers, and they interviewed each one of us, speaking only in German. I was first in the queue, and about 30 of my relatives were behind me. They were from both my mother's side and my father's side, but many of them I did not know well.

When I was called forward, I whispered to my mother and Anna, "Stay close by me." They stood behind me while I was questioned. It was more like an interrogation than an interview, and I didn't know if I was giving the right answers. The German interviewing me didn't look at me directly. He kept his eyes down, making notes.

"Where are you from?" he asked.

"Falenko, near Merefa in Ukraine," I said. "I've been working with the Ukrainian police there for about four months."

"What were your tasks with the police?"

"Keeping the peace and fighting the Russian partisans."

"I see," he said, moving his pen across the paper. "And what about your education?"

"I was in the second year at technical college when the war started."

He then looked at me with steely eyes. "Have you ever been a communist?"

There was a sharp intake of breath from my mother, audible only to me and my sister. I had been expecting this question. I knew if I said I'd ever been involved in any form of communism, I would be killed, but I could answer honestly. To me, being a Young Communist didn't equate to being a full communist.

"No, sir," I said calmly, looking him straight in the eye.

"Good," he said looking back at his notes, "and are you in general good health?"

"Yes, sir."

The final hurdle came when I was asked to drop my trousers for my penis to be checked. As I'd done this in the Russenlager, I knew I had nothing to fear, although the sense of humiliation was the same.

I stayed with my mother and sister while they were questioned too. In my favour was the fact that the Nazis still believed they could create an exclusively Aryan nation and were selecting people from different countries to join them. I had blond hair and also spoke some German. I was lucky—if I'd been classed as a foreigner, I would have been sent to a concentration camp. That's what happened to lots of the girls. Their heads were shaved immediately.

After the man had finished questioning my mother and Anna, he called across the hall to another German. "Hans, take these people to the station."

Hans escorted us to the train station. Although I thought the interview had gone fairly well, I had no idea where we were going or what fate lay in store for us. We never got to say goodbye to the rest of our relatives. For the moment, I was just glad the three of us had been able to stay together. The other former Ukrainian policemen and their families joined us.

To our immense surprise, we were put on a first-class train. It was fast and clean, with tables with tablecloths and white linen napkins. I'd never seen anything like it in my life. I didn't know why they were treating us like this. It was completely different from the goods train we'd been on previously.

It was the spring of 1943. No one told us anything about what we had been selected for. But I did know one thing: I didn't want to stay in Germany.

7

ON FIREMAN'S DUTY

My heart sank as the train pulled into the station and we were told to get out. We were in Heilbronn, 30 kilometres north of Stuttgart and still in Germany. I stood with Anna and my mother on the platform with the other former Ukrainian policemen and their families. I thought I was to be conscripted for the front line because I was just the right age.

Two men in Luftwaffe uniforms approached us, and one of them spoke. "Welcome to firemen's school," he said. "I'm Westina, your instructor. Your wives and families will be accommodated in a hostel nearby, but you need to come with me." The Germans didn't have enough people for the police or the fire brigade because they had sent all the young men to fight in the war. We were to replace the full-time firemen; we just had to do what we were told.

I hastily said goodbye to my mother and Anna, and then we marched to the marketplace in Heilbronn where the training centre was based. We were given a decent room with comfortable beds and white sheets. It was all so different from the Soviet Union. There were 12 of us altogether being trained in firefighting: 11 Ukrainians and, surprisingly, one Russian. He was a tall, well-built man, about 27 years old, who was terrified of being sent back to Russia. His Russian wife had been assigned to work in a German textile factory along with the other policemen's wives.

Westina was an excellent instructor who trained us well. Before we started, he gave us a warning: "You're under military law now. If you commit any misdemeanours, you can be tried in a military court rather than a civil one." This was because we had joined the Luftschutz (the air protection police) and wore Luftwaffe uniforms. This was no civilian fire brigade.

"In the most serious cases," Westina continued, "you could be sent to a slave labour camp."

No one fancied this prospect as it sounded too much like the Soviet Union. Consequently there were no problems with discipline. We were divided into three groups of four and given five or six months of intensive training. It was tough work, and we had to be physically strong to keep up. We had to assemble and dismantle apparatus of various sorts, and run with hoses that were tremendously heavy. There was also a great deal of marching: we would be in groups of four—links, rechts, left, right—and then we had to make a salute—"Heil Hitler!".

German fire engines were the most modern in the world, probably several years ahead of the ones then used in Britain. They included innovations like electric aluminium ladders. There was even a three-storey extendable ladder on one of the vehicles. Some of the ladders had a hook at one end which could be thrown on to a ledge and immediately gripped the surface. Every street had a water hydrant. All you had to do was connect the hydrant to the engine—another clever German system.

Many of the engines carried three fire hoses. At least two men were required to hold each hose, while a metal stand was often used to steady it. The hose was so powerful when under pressure that it could easily knock down a wall. When holding it, we had to rope ourselves to a wall otherwise we would have been pulled over. One of the engines sprayed foam instead of water on to fires involving petrol or oil.

Every German who had a business was a part-time fireman. Our driver, Schweike, sold all kinds of ironware. There was a cook called Otto who ran a butcher's shop. He travelled to Stuttgart,

Ludwigsburg and other places with a portable kitchen for the fire brigade. He had no children and treated me like a son. Westina, the head of training, ran an electrical engineering business. When he found out that I'd been a student electrician, he asked me to help him wire the police headquarters.

Part of Westina's job was to protect a large factory close by. Westina set up sheds around the factory which contained big barrels full of oil attached to a generator. When there was a daylight bombing raid, he would switch the generator on so that the oil made a huge plume of smoke. This meant the factory was shrouded every time the American bombers came over, and they never saw it. That lasted up until the spring of 1945. The factory survived the war and is now owned by Audi.

I became really pally with Westina, and he invited me to his house to meet his family. He had grapes growing on a hill, which I helped him to collect. By the end of the summer, I'd completed my training. As I'd done well in the fire training exams in September 1943, Westina recommended that I be put in charge of instructing a second group of 33 former Ukrainian policemen who had just arrived from Odessa. I was still only 18.

The Germans had requisitioned part of a factory in Heilbronn for the fire brigade, and I was transferred there. The garage was used for the fire engine, and there was a yard with washing facilities and a lavatory. In the factory, 50 or 60 girls were assembling one of Germany's secret weapons, V-1 flying bombs—doodlebugs as the people of Britain came to know them.

I had to keep discipline over the men I was training and followed Westina's example. I warned them about the military court. If they did something wrong, I charged them a penalty of one German mark. I never had to report anyone to the officials because discipline was good. There were a few daft ones who used to pick up cigarettes someone had dropped on the road while we were marching. That cost them one mark. I never asked to be the leader; I just had to do what I was told. The girls always liked it though. I became pretty friendly with one of the doodlebug girls called Freda. She was lovely.

One day in autumn 1943, I must have been really tired because I fell asleep inside the factory. I woke to the sound of an explosion. Shards of glass were flying everywhere and there was the terrible sound of steel and brick collapsing. It was a bombing raid on the factory. The shock waves blew out the windows and part of the roof. Everyone else had run into the shelter, but I hadn't heard the alarm. Luckily, the roof was still intact above me. My bed was right against a wall. If it had been further into the room, I would probably have been killed.

Eventually, our group of 12 was split up. One lot travelled to Untergruppenbach, while the other five and I were sent to Brackenheim, about 15 kilometres from Heilbronn. Here, we were working for a man called Weber. He was nothing like Westina. Aged about 35, Weber had been a manager or director of a department store. He should have been in the army, but he had somehow wangled an exemption. The Zugführer, we called him; it was the equivalent of being a platoon leader.

Weber only came once a day, before eight o'clock in the morning for five minutes, when he would give us our orders. All the firefighting training was stopped. Instead, we had to load and unload trains full of stones and bricks, and dig air-raid shelters for the population as well as for some individual houses such as Weber's. We helped with the harvest too. This had nothing to do with the fire brigade; Weber was just using us as free labour.

Mind you, with the increase in bombing raids, bunkers were hugely important, and we weren't the only ones digging. The German girls who worked at the doodlebug factory had to spend two hours after work each day digging bunkers, unpaid.

In Brackenheim, part of a dairy had been requisitioned for the fire brigade. We had two small rooms and a little office. I was in one room; the other five had bunk beds in another room. There were also washing facilities and a lavatory, and a garage for the fire engine.

Although I hadn't really wanted to go to Germany, I felt comfortable there. I was in a pleasant, clean environment. I wasn't frightened because I felt safe from the Russians in Germany. We were looked after—they gave us good food and we could take a bath every week. There was a special dining room for police and firemen, which we utilised every day. Waitresses (whom we called fräuleins) brought the food to our tables; we didn't even have to queue up for it.

In the morning, we sent a man to get ersatz coffee, which was made out of roasted corns not proper coffee beans. For breakfast, we had two slices of bread with jam and a bit of butter. We were each issued with a square aluminium tin with a lid, which we carried around with us. Our goulash lunch was put in this and there was always something similar in the evening, often with vegetables. At weekends, we had a roast meal, usually veal. We were also each given an aluminium water bottle. To drink, we had either water or Most—German cider.

Every Friday, we bathed at the big public baths between three and four in the afternoon. It was the first time I'd been to one of these places. The hot baths and showers were in separate cubicles, and you could choose to have one or the other. The

Germans looked after our health too. If any of us fell ill, we could visit a special clinic for the fire brigade and policemen.

I was paid five German marks a week in the fire brigade. With that, I could buy a packet of sugar, 40 cigarettes and two packets of tobacco. I didn't smoke and gave the cigarettes and tobacco to my mother. For us firemen, food was not an issue because we were classed as German. My mother was given a ration card. Nearby was the Knorr factory, where they made salamis and soup. There were 150 Italian prisoners of war working there, and they regularly stole food such as butter from the factory—they were very good thieves—but they couldn't get tobacco, so my mother was able to barter the cigarettes for extra food.

We wore a brown uniform with jackboots to work. For attending fires, there was a white canvas uniform with a black metal helmet and a leather neck piece and shoulder pieces. We also had a Luftwaffe uniform to wear on Sundays and at parades. There was a swastika emblem on the front of our black caps, the same as those worn by military regiments. The kit included a four-inch-wide leather belt with hooks, spare rope and an axe attached to it. We were each issued with a green metal-and-rubber gas mask, which was supposed to be carried at all times. As it was cumbersome in its metal box on a shoulder strap, I only took it with me when I was working. Once a year, I had to travel to Heilbronn to get the filters changed.

Outside work, I didn't mix with Ukrainians because most of my friends were German. They were always friendly towards me. That first Christmas in Germany, in 1943, Rosenberg, who ran the molkerei (dairy), invited me to the office on Boxing Day. He had two daughters. One was married with a child. Her husband was in the Wehrmacht. I was friendly with the younger one called Hedwig, who was unmarried. We listened to Hitler's speech on the radio and they treated me to Glühwein, a special hot wine with herbs. Hedwig always waited for me to come outside and we'd kiss around the corner. After the speech, we played Postman's Knock, the girls and me—a great kissing game.

About this time, my mother started to get anxious and wanted both my sister and me to find a spouse. One night, she came late to the dairy and brought a girl with her. My mother left her there and returned home. She wanted me to make love to the girl that night so that I would then marry her. This girl was a stranger to me, and I didn't know what to do. It was late. I told her to sleep in my bed. I didn't make love to her; I slept in the chair.

I didn't need my mother's help anyway as far as romance was concerned. There were many pretty girls in Brackenheim and Heilbronn, and I courted lots of them. I had many offers of marriage. All the young men had gone off to war, which was a factor in my favour. I was popular with the girls because I looked Aryan and I was now fluent in German.

This popularity did have a downside. I had to attend the clinic to get a special ointment because I made love to a German girl and I got crabs. I never knew her name.

Another time, I met a pretty German girl outside. She asked me to take a walk with her, she wanted to make love. Again, I never knew her name. Unfortunately, I got crabs again. I returned to the police clinic. "You again!" said the doctor. "Don't you even know the name of the girl?" I shook my head. After that, I was scared to death. I had learned my lesson.

Soon after this, I met Heidi Schweike. She was the niece of our German fire-engine driver, and she and her younger sister worked in his shop. They had lost their parents during the war. Heidi was brought to see me twice at the molkerei. Then she decided to come on her own. That's when it all started. Heidi was an extremely pretty girl, blonde and slim. I enjoyed spending time with her, and it wasn't long before it became more serious.

One evening, she came to see me and put a ring on my finger. She chose me, not the other way around. "Now we're engaged and you belong to me!" she said. I was only trying to be friendly, trying to improve my German, but I went along with it because she was so lovely.

Working for the fire brigade, we had to respond immediately if the alarm sounded. We often dealt with fires in Stuttgart. For instance, the Allies bombed a printing factory in the city where there were huge rolls of paper. When these became wet, it took at least a day before they dried out but then the paper ignited again. We had to stay all week because every time we extinguished the flames, the fire started again the following day.

Regularly, we also had to deal with fires in nearby Ludwigsburg, where there was a large car factory. Once, a train was bombed by the Americans and set ablaze. Even with the modern equipment we had, firefighting was dangerous work. In the other unit, two firemen died when they were tackling a blaze in a factory and the roof collapsed.

Once a year, there was a parade led by the Bürgermeister of Heilbronn. All the police and firemen were involved. We had to practise for weeks to get the marching right and the German songs correct as we had to sing and march at the same time. There was a band, and men from the army and navy as well as government officials took part in the parade. Five metres before reaching the Bürgermeister, we had to stop marching, salute, click our jackboots together and shout "Heil Hitler!". Then we had to do it again five metres after passing him.

The Germans had kept our family together. When my mother and sister first arrived in Heilbronn, they were in a hostel where over 100 different nationalities were accommodated. Then they were transferred to Sontheim, only two kilometres away, where 12 of the former Ukrainian policemen's wives worked in a textile factory. My mother lived in a sort of chalet and walked to Heilbronn every day. She and Anna worked there in the wäscherei (laundry) among Germans.

Wearing a Luftwaffe uniform helped me to fit in with the Germans. It also had an unwelcome effect: it identified me as an enemy to the Allies. On one occasion, in 1944, I was in Luftwaffe uniform walking along the street in Brackenheim. Out of nowhere, I heard a single-engined aeroplane approaching. When I looked up, I saw it was a British or American aircraft. Each wing had a machine gun or cannon and both fired at me simultaneously. They missed narrowly either side of me as I covered my head expecting the worst. After that my hair turned partly grey because I was so frightened and shaken.

On 4 December 1944, I was looking forward to a date with a girl at seven o'clock in the evening.

The British Royal Air Force had other ideas. It was the day of a huge bombing raid on Heilbronn when the city was almost completely destroyed. The sirens sounded 20 minutes before the planes came. As soon as the raid started, my colleagues and I were ordered to the communal bunker—the one we'd dug under Weber's command. There was a special area inside for us firemen.

The raid was unlike anything I'd experienced before. I could hear the horrible sound of the huge four-engined bombers. The ground shook, the din was indescribable. Around 500 aircraft were estimated to have dropped high-explosive bombs in the first attack. Half an hour later, another wave of aircraft released fire bombs, which seemed to suck up all the air.

The people who'd taken shelter in the cellars couldn't breathe and perished. The city was in ruins; the whole place was in flames.

The entire raid lasted no more than about 50 minutes. When we arrived later in Heilbronn, we were greeted by a horrific scene: the victims looked like jellyfish; all their facial features had melted under the heat of the flames.

There was not much we could do. Some had died in their houses while others had made it to the shelters. I didn't have to carry or touch the bodies, but I will never forget what they looked like. It was horrible. In less than an hour about 6–10,000 people were killed.[5]

Some bombs had been dropped on Brackenheim, where we were during the raid. If I'd been in Heilbronn proper, it's likely that I wouldn't be here today.

A few months later, in the spring of 1945, I was in Brackenheim outside a large civic building. In the distance, I could hear the faint sound of a single-engined aircraft. Thinking it was a German plane, I didn't turn to look at it. Suddenly, there was the clang of metal at my side. A small bomb had landed between the kerbstone and the pavement where I was standing. By instinct, I lay face down, flat on the pavement. A tall, thin man in a suit walking behind me remained standing. He was killed instantly when the bomb exploded. There wasn't much damage in the street, and just the top of my head was scorched by the heat of the explosion. This time it was the kerb that saved my life because it cushioned the blast.

After the bombing of Heilbronn, everyone was on tenterhooks because it was clear that the war had turned decisively in the Allies' favour. No one knew what was going to happen to the Germans or

---

5 *Initial estimates were of twice as many fatalities. Even the later, lower, and probably more accurate, figures nevertheless indicate a high mortality.*

to us Ukrainians who had worked for them. If Hitler was defeated, we were going to be on the losing side. Would the Germans be turfed out of their homes? Would the Russians return? It was a waiting game, one that kept us all awake at night.

8

AN UNCERTAIN FUTURE

Heilbronn finally fell to the Americans on 12 April 1945, nine days after the battle for the city had begun. We didn't know it at the time, but I was told later that it was the last place in the country to surrender to the Americans.

The Germans moved us Ukrainians who were in the fire brigade about 50 kilometres west of Heilbronn and left us on a big farm. Three fire engines were taken there too as we still had to respond to any fires, although none were reported. The other Ukrainians in the area who'd been in the police or the fire brigade were also assembled there.

There were about 40 of us altogether, all Ukrainian except for seven Germans, who were either drivers or field cooks. We had a field kitchen and, as it was summer, we slept in the hay in a barn with the chickens. We weren't told why we had been moved, but we knew what was going on because we listened to the radio. The waiting around was interminable.

It was the same German Zugführer—Weber—who came most days and gave us orders to remove large boulders and stones from the farmer's field. He would turn up in the morning for around an hour before driving off. This was done to keep us busy, gainfully employed and disciplined. All weapons were put in a pile bearing a white flag. We knew that the Americans were about five kilometres away. We waited a week to ten days for those Americans to come.

When they finally arrived, in their jeeps and lorries, they looked scared and anxious. There were only about 30 American soldiers, and they had been reluctant to get too close until reinforcements arrived. They were extremely young, and perhaps they thought there would be more Germans than there were. Although few in number, they were well equipped, and I was scared of them.

One of the Americans spoke in German. "Who's in charge?"

No one answered, so I stepped forward. "I am," I said.

The American soldier nodded. There was no further conversation. We were now their prisoners of war, and they shouted at us to form a line.

Presumably, as we were still wearing our brown uniforms with jackboots, they thought we were all German, not Ukrainian.

We had to walk about half a kilometre while the Americans guarded us with their guns. By midday, we reached a huge schloss—a castle—and were forced into a large wine cellar. There were other prisoners already in there, making a total of about 200 Ukrainians and Germans all mixed in together. Several American soldiers guarded the cellar from above with grenades and machine guns. I was scared to death in case they dropped the grenades on us.

While we were in the cellar, the women from the local area were put upstairs in the castle. Their shouts and cries echoed through the building. They were being raped by the Americans. The screaming continued for hours. It was harrowing to hear what was happening, and to be powerless to do anything. I tried to close my eyes and cover my ears. It didn't shut out the screaming. There's no justice in war.

When it had all gone quiet, we were ordered out of the cellar and marched to a prison camp about three kilometres away. We were prisoners of war, living in a field like animals for a couple of days. We had to sleep on the grass with no shelter at all—just as I had in the Russenlager back in Ukraine. There was no sanitation, and we were given only stale bread and water. I was hungry but not starving. The

American soldiers guarded us by creating an outer circle with their tanks and jeeps. We had no idea what was going to happen next. It turned out that this small camp was just the calm before the storm.

After a couple of days, we had to march for several hours to a bigger open-air prisoner of war camp, where I was held for two long months. During this time, no questions were asked and no one knew what was in store for us. In this camp, there were several hundred POWs. They seemed to consist of those who the Americans thought were German and in a position of authority. I was probably among them because I looked Aryan, spoke German and I'd said I was in charge of the firemen.

Like the smaller camps, there was no perimeter fence, although there was an American outer circle made up of sentries with machine guns, jeeps and guard towers. We all had to wear the clothes we'd arrived in and again there was no shelter, just the grass to sleep on. There were no drains, toilet facilities or toilet paper; we simply had to find a place to go on the grass. Luckily, it did not rain all summer, but because of the heat the smell was awful.

We were given water and some food, which was thrown out of the back of a jeep three times a day—stale bread, salty sardines and peanut butter. It was a bit like feeding time at the zoo because there was a mad scramble for food. Again, I was hungry but not starving. There was no laundry, medicine or doctors. We weren't made to work, meaning there was nothing to do all day except sit and wait, and sleep.

After two months, the Americans started processing the prisoners. I was called into the office, where two soldiers sat behind a desk. One spoke to me in German.

"We'd like you to sign this form," he said, pointing to a document on the desk.

"Why do I need to sign that?" I didn't look at the papers because I wanted a straight answer to my question.

"We want you to join the American army," he said. "If you sign the form, after four years you'll become an American citizen and you'll be able to stay in America."

I knew the Americans were still fighting the Japanese, and I'd had enough of the war. "I'm sorry, I can't," I said.[6] "I have a mother and sister living in Sontheim, and I'm engaged to a German woman."

It was at this point that they realised I was Ukrainian, not German.

---

6 Had Wolodymyr accepted, he would have had the remarkable record of having been, in just over four years, twice conscripted into the Soviet forces, once conscripted into the German forces, and then recruited into the American forces plus also, on separate occasions, being a POW of the Germans and of the Americans.

After my refusal to sign the form, I was allowed to leave the camp. I walked back to Sontheim, which was about 20 kilometres away. It took all day to get there and I had little food. Although the war had ended, my problems were just beginning.

Nearby Heilbronn was still a disaster zone, with rubble everywhere. But neither the laundry nor the power station had been destroyed because they were on the outskirts near the River Neckar. When I returned after two months, I couldn't find Heidi. The shop was there and all her family, but she had left. Her uncle wouldn't tell me where she was. I suspected she'd found an American boyfriend.

I had another unwelcome surprise when I visited my mother and sister in Sontheim. They were outside the chalet, and standing with them was a young Russian officer, a lieutenant who until recently had been a German prisoner of war.

As I approached, I was painfully conscious of the fact that I was still wearing my German Luftwaffe uniform with a swastika on the cap. The Russians could hang me for that. My mother introduced the Russian officer as Anna's boyfriend. We shook hands briefly. Nothing was said between us.

The Russian was of medium height, slim with dark hair, and handsome. He was wearing a brand new brown Russian army uniform, jackboots and a hat with a red star on the front. He had a pistol in a holster. I was unarmed. Although I had only just met him, I instinctively didn't like or trust him. I was scared of him as I knew he had the power to hand my mother, Anna and me over to the Russian authorities.

I didn't stay long. Before I left my mother gave me most of her German money. "We're all heading east to make a new start," she said. She couldn't take the German money with her to Russia.

I couldn't believe what I was hearing. After all we had been through escaping from the Soviet Union, now Mother was going back voluntarily.

My sister was young—only 16—and it was obvious she was very much in love. She was also stupid because she thought she could stay with her soldier boyfriend. I suspected they would be separated straightaway and that he would be returned to the army. I believe my mother thought that the Russian officer could protect them. I was not going to start discussing the situation while he was there, so I left.

With the money my mother gave me I rented decent digs in Heilbronn, paying for a whole month upfront. As I was in Luftwaffe uniform, it was easy for me to get a job as an electrician at the power station.

Not long afterwards, Anna and my mother were rounded up by the Russians, put on the back of a lorry and taken to a camp which had previously been a German barracks. An agreement had been made with Britain, America and France for Stalin to collect everyone from the Soviet Union and return them home. I didn't want to go back because I'd worked for the Germans and I knew what would happen if I did. I would have either been shot or sent to a Gulag camp.

At first, people were allowed to come and go freely from the camp. Mother came to see me at my digs two nights in a row. On the first evening that she came, I gave her my Luftwaffe overcoat with my engagement ring in the pocket.

"This is a new Luftwaffe uniform," I said. "There's no mark on it. It's good quality. You'd better take it because you know how cold it can get in Ukraine." I handed it to her, pointing out the contents of the pocket.

She took it and then said suddenly, "Come with us, Wolodymyr. We can be a family again."

"You know I can't," I said. "If I go with you, I'll either be shot or sent for at least 25 years' hard labour behind barbed wire, which would be the same as being dead. I would be separated from you straightaway in any case."

She nodded sadly.

"It is you that has to make a choice," I said. "You can stay with me or go with Anna."

"Anna is so young," Mother said. "She needs me more than you do. Besides, her boyfriend will protect us."

I shook my head. In my heart, I knew she'd already decided to go with my sister.

The next day—the last day I saw my mother—she told me about some fancy coats she'd acquired. I didn't ask how she'd got them, although I had my suspicions. At the time, people were looting the German warehouses. She had probably bought them on the black market, hoping to be able to exchange them for food as she'd done when we left Ukraine.

On the third day Mother did not come. I found out afterwards that she and Anna had been put on to a freight train and sent east. Everyone was expecting it, but I was not able to say goodbye properly. That was the last I heard of them. There were no letters, nothing.

The Germans were good to Ukrainians like me. They would hide us from the Russians and say we were working for them, for example. Two months after Mother left, I visited the laundry where she had worked. I asked the boss if he would give me some papers because I was afraid that if the Russians caught me, they would shoot me. He knew me because my mother had worked there for two years. He was helpful and gave me documents that said I was a stoker at the laundry. This was security for me in case I was caught by the Russians. Luckily, I never had to show those papers to anyone.

The food situation in Germany was now dire because millions of displaced people, including Poles, Estonians, Yugoslavs, Russians and Ukrainians, refused to return home. No one wanted to go back to communism. Moreover, Stalin was suspicious of all those who had seen the West, even if they had been prisoners of war or forced labourers. There were probably some 11 million such foreigners in Germany. There was little food, even for the Germans, and nothing in the shops. I could eat only in a restaurant. Even then, it was just soup made of cabbage or potato and 200 grams of bread a day with my ration card. Nobody can live on that. Many German girls courted Americans in the hope of marriage, often just because they wanted to survive.

I had a good friend called Ivan, a Ukrainian who was born about 15 kilometres from my village. During the war, Ivan had lost a brother and sister. I first met him when we were in the Ukrainian police under German occupation, and I had to visit the headquarters in Chutove for shooting practice from time to time. Ivan and I had a great deal in common: We were both in the German fire brigade. He'd been sent to Untergruppenbach while I'd gone to Brackenheim. My mother and his mother were friends.

After my mother left Germany to return to the Soviet Union, Ivan's mother and father decided to look after me. I left the power station and began working with Ivan in Untergruppenbach. There was a turnhalle (sports hall) that had been requisitioned by firemen during the war. Ivan and I lived there with his parents. We both found work with the local council, cutting trees down in the forest. There we worked with a huge saw, two Ukrainians with two Germans, two on one side and two on the other. We were cutting thick trees suitable for house building. Anyone could buy any leftover wood.

It was easier to find food in the villages, and we could get extra work on the land and be paid in food. The Americans used to empty all kinds of waste food on to a scrap heap, and Ivan's parents found butter and bread just by being observant.

In the winter, we cut trees in the woods; in the summer, we worked in a sawmill. An attractive married lady called Maria Preis picked me out from all the Germans and Ukrainians to collect wood for her and tie it up, ready for the winter. She was well off with a big house and farm and a couple of children.

Maria's husband had fought with the Wehrmacht at Stalingrad and was missing, presumed dead. She wrote letters to the Russian Red Cross, to the Kremlin, to every place possible in Russia to try to find out about her husband, never receiving an answer.

From time to time, she invited me to her house. First, it was once a week, then twice a week; I played with the children and she gave me good food. After a while, she asked me to marry her.

"You'll have a big house and a wife," she said. "You won't find a better situation than that."

She was lovely, and I said yes.

Sadly, as she couldn't prove her husband had been killed, her father-in-law wouldn't let us marry. He told her she would have to wait until ten years had passed. That put an end to any talk of marriage. I made love to her once, and she asked me to move in with her. I should have done it but I hesitated. That was a mistake. Maria was a few years older than me. She was also extremely pretty—the prettiest woman in that area.

By the winter of 1945/46, there were increasing numbers of refugees in Germany with insufficient accommodation for them all. A commissioner would inspect private houses. If somebody had six rooms, he was allowed to keep four but he would be compelled to reserve the other two for refugees.

It was also becoming increasingly dangerous for us because the Russians had stepped up their efforts to have their people returned to the Soviet Union. Stalin was both cunning and paranoid. He knew of the huge numbers of Ukrainians who had served in the German army or had been working in Germany. He was fearful that what they had seen of the West would have illuminated the deficiencies of communism. If they were returned, they could be sent to the Gulag slave-labour camps.

The Russians were allowed the freedom to travel anywhere they wanted to collect their people without the Americans intervening. Russian interrogators would come to a village, ask about people's nationalities, and, if they felt like it, send them back to the Soviet Union by force. Under Stalin's agreement with the Americans, French and British to return former Soviet citizens to the East, more than 2 million were sent back. Some returned voluntarily. Most did not. Thousands committed suicide rather than return to Russia. It took two years before the Americans understood why people didn't want to return to the Soviet Union.

The Germans in Untergruppenbach tried to protect us. They knew what happened to those who travelled back to Russia because of how the Germans had been treated during the war. Many Poles, Russians and Ukrainians had replaced the farmers who'd been sent to fight and they had helped to keep German agriculture going. The Germans were grateful for this and told the Russian investigators that they had no foreigners on their farms, even though there were lots of Poles and Russians working there. Even the Russian who was in the fire brigade and was afraid to go back to Russia was given a job on a farm by the Germans. Despite this, we all became increasingly fearful for our safety. It was surely only a matter of time before we were discovered.

9
IN SEARCH OF SAFETY

The German people were good to us; they saved many Ukrainians. However, the situation was becoming increasingly stressful for us as we knew we could be picked up at any time by the Russians. Although the Germans had hidden us so far, there was only so much they could do.

I was determined not to go back. I remembered how my father had worked the system to survive under the communist regime, and I decided to try to do the same. The only way I could think of to ensure that I could not be deported by the Russians was to change my nationality. At that time I held a German passport, and I could have applied to be declared a German born in another country. But Germany had been defeated and had a tarnished reputation. I chose instead to be a Pole.

In order to do this, I went with Ivan to the Polish consulate in Stuttgart, where I had to tell a little white lie to the official who interviewed me. The Ukrainian provinces of Eastern Galicia and Volhynia had been under Polish rule until the Soviet invasion of 1939. A person born there in 1925 would have been a Polish national by birth.

"I was born in Volhynia," I told him. "Unfortunately, I was working in Heilbronn at the time of an air raid and all my papers and possessions went up in smoke."

"I see," he said. "And how can I help you?"

"I wonder if you would be kind enough to give me documentation to prove I'm Ukrainian-Polish?" I asked.

"Where in Volhynia were you born?" the ambassador said. "Have a look at the map on the wall here." He was clearly helping me, even though he'd worked out that I wasn't really Polish. But the Poles and Russians were bitter enemies, and he knew he was doing me a favour; this documentation would almost guarantee my freedom. I looked carefully at the map and pointed to a place called Zaluzie.

"That's good enough for me," he said and signed the papers certifying that I was Polish by birth. I still have these documents. It was on that day that my surname was changed to the Polish spelling of Papuca, rather than Papucia.

By mid-1946, the Americans finally came to understand why people were refusing to return to the Soviet Union. A series of so-called displacement camps were set up to protect the people who would not go home. Many of these camps were sited in buildings previously used by the German army. These camps were guarded by American troops, night and day. The Americans now also prevented the Russians from rounding up people from the countryside to send east.

Despite my new nationality, I was still in some danger from the Russians. By the summer, things had also become more desperate with regard to food supplies.

"Let's seek sanctuary in one of the new camps," I said to Ivan and his parents. "We'll be safe there and there might be more food."

They all agreed. There was no selection procedure, and the Americans didn't ask if you were Russian or who you were. They didn't know what to do; they just wanted to stop the suicides. The nearest American camp to Heilbronn was 120 kilometres east in a small town called Ellwangen near Württemberg. It had been a military base and barracks for German soldiers, and the site covered at least ten acres.

Altogether, there were about 4,500 men, women and children of all ages in the camp, including professors, teachers and other intellectuals.

They were mainly Ukrainians. There were also some Russians and Yugoslavs. The Poles had a separate camp elsewhere. We felt safe there, and we were free to come and go from the camp because we were in the American Zone of Germany, protected by their tanks and troops. The American Zone covered a third of Germany, all of Bavaria, Baden, Württemberg and Heidelberg.

A wall ran around the entire perimeter of the camp at Ellwangen, and the accommodation was in two-storey stone buildings. Single men and women lived in same sex dormitories and each person was allocated a bunk bed. There were showers and baths and a communal kitchen. There was a sickbay, which luckily I never had to use. There were many grassy areas, previously used for parking military vehicles, where we could play football and volleyball.

The only problem—and it was a big problem— was the food. I had been wrong in thinking we would get more in the camp. Breakfast was potato or cabbage soup with bread; lunch was only bread, 200g per person; and dinner was soup again. There was just enough food to survive on, that's all.

People from all over the world sent us clothes, shoes and food via charities like the Red Cross, but there was a lot of corruption at the camp. Ukrainians from West Ukraine were put in charge of food and clothes distribution. They stole many of the things meant for us, and sold them on the black market. People sent chocolate bars and all sorts of delicacies. We never saw any of them. The only donation I ever received was a coat. Many of these corrupt Ukrainians moved to Canada. They had presumably made so much money that they were easily able to buy land and property.

In the camp we stuck together with a group of other Ukrainians we'd known in the fire brigade. There were 13 of us altogether. My time in the camp at Ellwangen was reasonably happy, and I made many friends there. Many of these also travelled to Canada eventually.

After a couple of months I was able to resume my studies. The university professors ran a school inside the camp called the Ukrainian Gymnasium. It was similar to a grammar school. This education was paid for by UNESCO (the United Nations Educational, Scientific and Cultural Organisation) and anyone could choose to study there.

I had the highest grades in the class because I had already completed nine years out of ten of my education. The course lasted a whole year from 1946 to 1947, with no more than 17 students per class. I had little spare time as it was all taken up with study. The school day was from eight in the morning until four in the afternoon, and I had lots of homework. On top of that, I was selected to teach maths in the evenings to others who were often the same age as me. For this I was paid a small amount. With this and the money I gained from selling my ration of chocolate, when I had some, I bought books on chemical engineering from the German bookshop in the town.

At Ellwangen, I learned Latin for the first time. Latin was then essential for acceptance at university. I had to memorise pages and pages of the writings of Julius Caesar and repeat them, either orally or in writing. I also learned English in this one year. I understood the grammar pretty well, although my spelling was awful. I had other lessons in Ukrainian and German, both languages I spoke already.

Those who were more practical and less academic, without good grades, could complete a two-year apprenticeship within the camp. This consisted of building, plumbing and electrical work. While I was studying, some of the other people in the camp did cleaning work in the kitchen and other jobs. They were paid for this work, the money coming from UNESCO.

In 1946, while I was living in the camp, with a group of 12 others I visited Hitler's Eagle's Nest mountaintop base at Berchtesgaden near Salzburg. All Russian soldiers had left this part of Germany, and we felt safe enough to make the day trip. We travelled there by train. The rail network was electrified and still working, in spite of the damage caused during the war.

When we arrived at the pretty town of Berchtesgaden, the American troops would not let us use the tunnel or the lift that had been constructed inside of the mountain to Eagle's Nest. We were undeterred and decided to climb the route behind the mountain instead. The five-hour climb, often up sheer rock, was foolhardy and dangerous. We were determined to get to the top anyway, despite having no mountaineering gear. At the summit, we met more American troops. They took no notice of us. The base was vast, made of natural grey stone with balconies giving fantastic views across the Alps. Most of it had been stripped. There was just the odd gun emplacement left. The troops and other day trippers had already started to scratch their names in charcoal on the walls.

On another occasion, I enjoyed a boat trip down the Danube. This was a lovely day because it took me out of the daily routine at the camp and helped me to forget my fear of the future.

Another day trip was less joyful. We travelled to the border with Czechoslovakia, where we watched the Russian border guards from a safe distance.

It was a sombre day because we reflected on our friends and family who had been forced to go east. This made me emotional and angry, knowing that I was unlikely to see my homeland, my mother or sister again.

At the Ukrainian Gymnasium, I had the highest marks for everything except languages. I was especially good at chemistry. Two of the teachers selected me to attend Regensburg University in 1947 to study chemistry on a five-year course funded by UNESCO. Sadly, there weren't enough teachers or lecturers and it never happened. The priority was to open schools for younger children.

Life had by now become almost unbearable at Ellwangen because of the lack of food. I was getting thin, and I felt I couldn't stay any longer. The war had devastated Germany, and the only work available was in construction. Although I really liked Germany and wished to stay, I knew that if I wanted to ensure my survival I would have to move again.

10
ENGLAND CALLING

The authorities at Ellwangen had started trying to disperse people, and a noticeboard appeared advertising some job opportunities in other countries. The first one I saw was for a lumberjack in Canada. This sounded right up my street because I'd been a lumberjack in the forest in Germany. Ivan applied as well. I was excited about the prospect, but it turned out that 350 people applied for 50 jobs. I wasn't one of the lucky ones and neither was Ivan.

Another notice appeared, this time for a draughtsman in the Venezuelan oilfields. Again, this was a job I was well qualified to do and I applied for it. After three weeks I had not heard anything. Then I saw a notice asking for people to work in factories in England. It was a scheme organised by the British government. Although these weren't skilled jobs,

I knew that Britain was an industrial country and there might be further work opportunities for me there. I had learned to speak English at school in Ellwangen, so I applied.

Ivan wanted to try his luck in England too. He wasn't able to because the authorities would only accept single men without families and he wanted to take his parents with him. They waited another two years, then they moved to Canada, where Ivan changed his name to John.

My request to travel to Britain was granted. That was just the first stage in the process. I had to pass three medical examinations before my application could be finalised: the first was at the camp in Ellwangen, another in Stuttgart and the final one in Münster. They were checking carefully for any signs of illness; you couldn't enter Britain if you had an infectious disease.

Luckily, I passed all the medical tests. I was given a certificate of identity in lieu of a passport from the office of the military governor in the American Zone of Germany. My nationality was listed again as Ukrainian, not Polish—at last I could tell the truth. I also received some help from the Ukrainian Service for Counsel and Aid in Augsburg, which gave me a certificate to prove who I was. On the reverse, it said I was stateless because I had refused to return to the Soviet Union.

I was the first from the Ellwangen camp to leave for Britain. The only things I knew about the country were those I'd been taught in school. I didn't expect anything when I left Germany. I wasn't scared because it was just a new opportunity. Most importantly, I knew I would be safe.

Within a fortnight of applying, I was put on an old warship which was also carrying prisoners of war and discharged soldiers. I reached England on 22 December 1947. In 1953 I became a British citizen.

In 1990, with the fall of communism, I wrote to the councillor of my village in Ukraine. He used to be a headteacher in Horlivka and his name was Shevchenko (although he wasn't related to me). He confirmed that if I'd returned home after the war, I would have been given at least 15 years' hard labour. Shevchenko visited the archives in Kharkov. The name Papucia was in the register and they still remembered my family, but he only found records relating to my family from before the war, not during it or afterwards. Sadly, after some of the Ukrainians found out I lived in England, they thought I was earning lots of money and many people pretended to be my relatives to try to get their hands on some of it. I became fed up with it.

Then in 2000, a Ukrainian student called Andre came to Britain and I met him. He was from the same part of Ukraine as I was. As his father had been in charge of the collective farms, he knew what had happened during and after the war. He told me there was no one left from my family. Nobody had gone home from Germany to the Falenko area with the exception of one Ukrainian policeman, who'd also been a fireman in Germany. When he returned, the Soviets sentenced him to many years' hard labour. My mother and sister never made it home. They must also have been sent to a Siberian slave camp. In my heart, I always knew that this was what had happened, otherwise they would have got in touch somehow. Still, it broke my heart to have this confirmed. The village of Falenko was apparently completely destroyed in the war and is no longer marked on maps.

When I look back at the things that my family and I had to do and the decisions that had to be made merely to survive, I don't think politicians realise that their actions have such devastating and long-lasting repercussions. They often do things which cannot be undone for many years if at all. It was 50 years after I left before I felt I could safely visit Ukraine. But as I write this, the area I lived in has been turned into a war zone once again, and the homeland I knew in my childhood is unrecognisable.

Although my roots will always be in Ukraine, Britain is my home now. It is a place where I was made welcome, where I could enjoy my freedom, live without fear, and build a life for my family. To many people, this would be unremarkable. To me, it is everything.

MAP 1

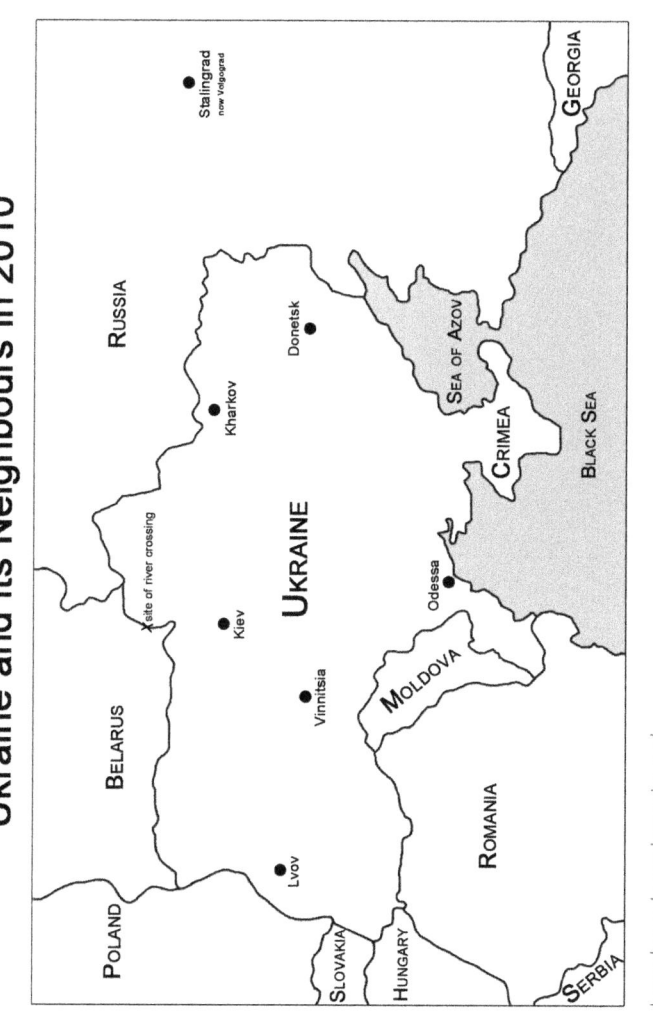

Ukraine and its Neighbours in 2010

MAP 2

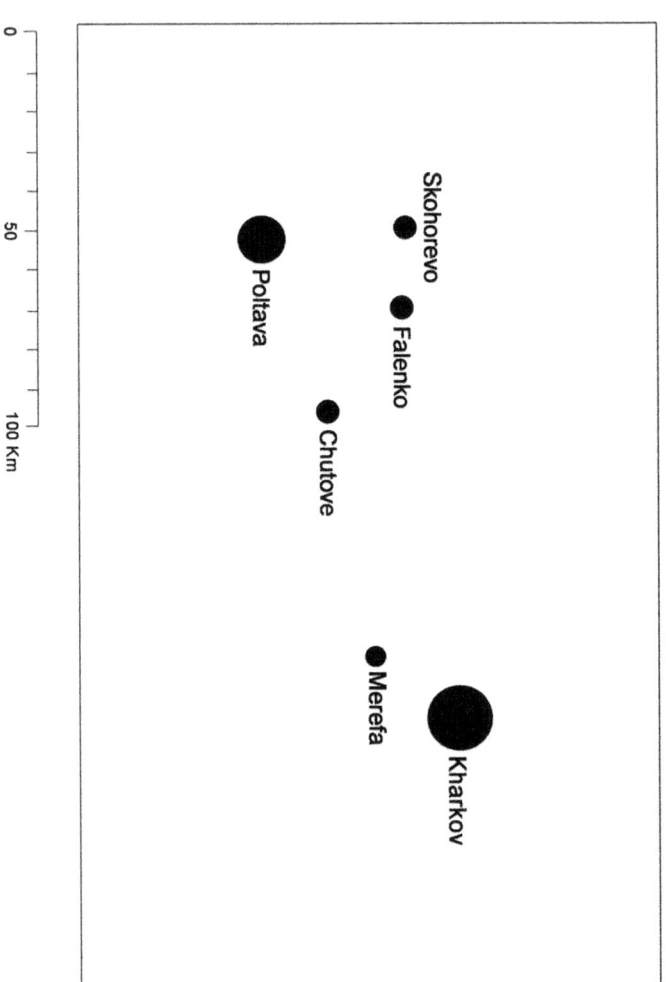

MAP 3

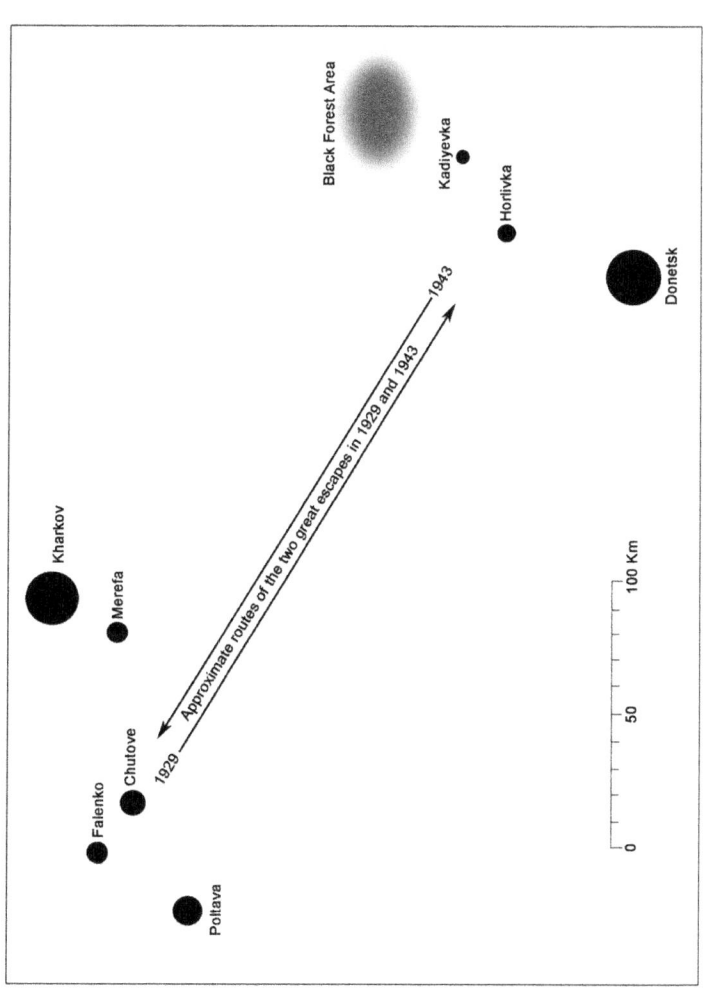

Black Forest Area

Kadiyevka

Horlivka

Donetsk

Kharkov

Merefa

1943

Approximate routes of the two great escapes in 1929 and 1943

1929

Falenko

Chutove

Poltava

100 Km

50

0

Lightning Source UK Ltd.
Milton Keynes UK
UKOW07f0231210217
294905UK00011B/45/P